Taixu's "On the Establishment of the Pure Land in the Human Realm"

Also Available from Bloomsbury:

A Critique of Western Buddhism, Glenn Wallis

Chinese Familism, Jordan Paper

Dynamism and the Ageing of a Japanese New Religion, Erica Baffelli and Ian Reader

Taixu's "On the Establishment of the Pure Land in the Human Realm"

A Translation and Study

Charles B. Jones

BLOOMSBURY ACADEMIC
LONDON • NEW YORK • OXFORD • NEW DELHI • SYDNEY

BLOOMSBURY ACADEMIC
Bloomsbury Publishing Plc
50 Bedford Square, London, WC1B 3DP, UK
1385 Broadway, New York, NY 10018, USA
29 Earlsfort Terrace, Dublin 2, Ireland

BLOOMSBURY, BLOOMSBURY ACADEMIC and the Diana logo are trademarks of
Bloomsbury Publishing Plc

First published in Great Britain 2021
This paperback edition published 2022

Copyright © Charles B. Jones, 2021

Charles B. Jones has asserted his right under the Copyright, Designs and Patents Act, 1988, to be identified as Author of this work.

For legal purposes the Acknowledgments on pp. viii–ix constitute an extension of this copyright page.

Cover design and illustration © Rebecca Heselton

All rights reserved. No part of this publication may be reproduced or transmitted in any form or by any means, electronic or mechanical, including photocopying, recording, or any information storage or retrieval system, without prior permission in writing from the publishers.

Bloomsbury Publishing Plc does not have any control over, or responsibility for, any third-party websites referred to or in this book. All internet addresses given in this book were correct at the time of going to press. The author and publisher regret any inconvenience caused if addresses have changed or sites have ceased to exist, but can accept no responsibility for any such changes.

A catalogue record for this book is available from the British Library.

Library of Congress Control Number: 2020947727

ISBN: HB: 978-1-3501-4056-1
PB: 978-1-3502-0125-5
ePDF: 978-1-3501-4057-8
eBook: 978-1-3501-4427-9

Typeset by Newgen KnowledgeWorks Pvt. Ltd., Chennai, India

To find out more about our authors and books visit www.bloomsbury.com and sign up for our newsletters

For my parents
David R. Jones
Mary B. Jones
For long years of encouragement and support

Taixu (1890–1947). Illustration by Chenoa Hyson.

Contents

Preface and Acknowledgments	viii
Part One Introductory Study	1
1 Introduction	3
2 Taixu's Life to 1926	7
3 Previous Western Writings on Taixu's Ideas about the "Pure Land in the Human Realm"	31
4 Utopianism East and West in Taixu's Essay	37
5 Key Themes	49
Part Two The Translation	55
6 The Translation: On the Establishment of the Pure Land in the Human Realm	57
Part Three The Pure Land in the Human Realm after Taixu and Conclusions	127
7 The Pure Land in the Human Realm after Taixu	129
8 Concluding Remarks	141
Works Cited	145
Index	151

Preface and Acknowledgments

I conceived the idea for this book when I decided to read Taixu's essay "On the Establishment of the Pure Land in the Human Realm" (*Jianshe renjian jingtu lun* 建設人間淨土論) for myself. For some time, I had been studying the history of the Pure Land Buddhist tradition in China from ancient times to the twentieth century. In the course of this research, I found that the idea of creating a "Pure Land in the Human Realm" (*renjian jingtu* 人間淨土) had currency among Buddhist modernizers of the Republican period (1911–49), and this particular text seemed to be its *fons et origo*. Academic studies on Ven. Taixu (太虛, 1890–1947) always mentioned it and many provided highlights from it, and from these I got the impression that Taixu coined the term to criticize his fellow Buddhists for giving up on the present world and waiting passively for rebirth in the western Pure Land of the Buddha Amitābha. He argued that they should instead take up the cause of social and political reform and engage in welfare and relief work to make *this* world a pure land. In fact, the image of Taixu as a reformer and modernizer was so dominant in the scholarly imagination that both specialists and nonspecialists interpreted all of Taixu's ideas, including those found in the Essay, exclusively in its light.

Thus, the first time I read it, I was very surprised to find that it little resembled the clarion call to social engagement that I was expecting. It maintained a traditional picture of the Buddhist cosmos, quoted scriptures extensively, and devoted only a modicum of space to promoting social and political action. As a result, I decided to translate the work in full, not omitting the lengthy sutra passages and citations from other ancient religious classics that dominate several sections. Given the number of scholars who currently study either Buddhism in the Republican period or the movement known both as "Humanistic Buddhism" and "Engaged Buddhism," it seemed desirable that this text be available in English.

This was a team effort. I want to acknowledge first of all the help that Dr. Richard K. Payne of the Institute of Buddhist Studies gave me in affirming the timeliness of this translation and in connecting me with the present publisher. Dr. Eric Goodell, a specialist in Taixu studies and graduate school classmate, was always available to discuss everything from translation issues to general concepts, and for that I am grateful. Dr. Peter Zarrow of the University of Connecticut provided much-needed pointers and resources on political discourse during the early Republican period, in particular the thorny term "going red" (*chihua* 赤花). Dr. Jonathan Chaves of George Washington University helped with the interpretation of Taixu's verses. The collective entity known as the Sinologists Facebook group jumped in to guide me with other questions. I would also like to express my sincere thanks to Professor Chen Chienhuang 陳劍鍠 of the Centre for the Study of Humanistic Buddhism in the Chinese University of Hong Kong for making available to me his research on Ven. Xingyun while it was still in press. The anonymous manuscript reviewers provided good pointers and advice, and the final product is much improved by their input. I hope that this volume may prove useful to them and to others, and that in providing this translation I may repay their kindness. Finally, my parents poured forth love and support throughout my career, and I dedicate this book to them.

Part One

Introductory Study

1
Introduction

For scholars who study twentieth-century Chinese Buddhism, Ven. Taixu (太虛, 1890–1947) needs no introduction. He is widely regarded as one of the "four eminent monks" of the late Qing and early Republican periods, and, like his three companions on this list, he stands for a particular aspect of Buddhist life. Taixu is lionized as the preeminent exponent of modernization and reform. Hongyi (弘一, 1880–1942) epitomizes *vinaya* study and monastic reform. Xuyun (虛雲, 1840–1959) stands for meditation and the Chan School. Finally, Yinguang (印光, 1861–1940) appears as the driving force behind the Pure Land revival. While this makes for a neat scheme in which each of four general areas of Buddhist activity has its own figurehead, it creates obstacles for a proper understanding of them as individuals by inclining us to see each man only within the sphere of activity with which he has been identified while obscuring his other endeavors. Xuyun, for instance, did much more than meditate during his exceedingly long life. He also fostered monastic reform and helped direct the renovation of old temples. Yinguang spearheaded a major revival of Pure Land practice to be sure, but he also actively engaged in fundraising and publishing (see Kiely 2017). Besides this, the scheme distracts us from the associations these men had with each other and the great areas of overlap in their activities. Hongyi may be the man associated with *vinaya* study, but all four of these men, and many others besides, engaged in efforts to reform a monastic establishment widely seen as backward, corrupt, parasitic, and irrelevant.

We are thus liable to misapprehend Taixu's life and work if we see him only through the lens of modernization and reform. This became especially apparent to me when, in the course of pursuing research in Chinese Pure Land Buddhism, I read his essay "On the Establishment of the Pure Land in the Human Realm" (*Jianshe renjian jingtu lun* 建設人間淨土論, hereafter the "Essay") for the first time. Influenced by modern usages of the term "the Pure Land in the Human Realm" (*renjian jingtu* 人間淨土) in Taiwan and mainland China as well as in several academic studies, I expected to see Taixu the modernizer on full display. Specifically, I expected to see him use this long essay to discourage the Buddhists of his day from engaging in traditional Pure Land practice, to tell them not to be passive in the face of social and political upheaval, and to not pin all their hopes on rebirth in a distant buddha-land after they died. Instead, I thought he would push them to work within this world to make it a pure land by engaging in social welfare work, political reform, and activism of all sorts understood within a modern scientific worldview. This is what previous scholars had said he was interested in. This is what historians of modern Chinese religion had led me to expect.

The Essay upended these expectations. While calls to activism and reform work are not absent, they occupy surprisingly little space within it. Long quotations from traditional Buddhist sutras and other ancient religious literature make up a good deal of its content (the longest quotation takes up a full 18 percent of the Essay's space). He most emphatically does *not* discourage anyone from cultivating very traditional Pure Land practices or from aspiring to rebirth in Amitābha's buddha-land after they die. His ideas for creating the "Pure Land in the Human Realm" extend to several kinds of activity: from seeking rebirth in a Buddhist paradise such as Uttarakuru to purifying the present world through reform activities; from improving peoples' lives by fostering technological innovation to establishing a utopian mountaintop Buddhist community in which esoteric rituals for the welfare of the nation would have an important place. Furthermore, the Essay is unapologetic in its espousal of many premodern ideas, belying the scholarly shibboleth that he included traditional elements in his preaching simply as a sop to the ignorant masses (see, for example, Reichelt 1954, 152–7).

Some recent academic studies of Taixu have begun to peer behind Taixu's image to see him in a more rounded and nuanced way. I hope that this study and the translation of his Essay will help propel our understanding further along this path. In the chapters that form the preliminary study, we will first give a short overview of Taixu's life up to 1926, focusing in particular on events and publications that point toward the ideas presented in his Essay, and highlighting the influence that others had on the formation of its proposals. After that, I will review past Western academic and journalistic accounts of Taixu's life and thought, showing how his image as a modernizer and reformer led scholars to ignore or explain away the more traditional elements of his thought and activities. Following that, I will analyze the sources of the utopian vision that pervades the Essay, focusing on the distinction between utopias and paradises and the way that Taixu blended these two types of idealized lands into a single vision in order to overcome the problems inherent in each when implemented alone. The following chapter will highlight the major themes of the Essay.

After the translation, I will provide a brief description of the ways in which Taixu's concept of the Pure Land in the Human Realm fared after his death. The reader will see that it became a very elastic term capable of designating a variety of ideas and agendas, and that few of the modern proponents of this concept hew strictly to Taixu's vision. A concluding chapter will summarize the main themes and arguments that I wish to advance.

I hope that by translating Taixu's Essay in full, interested readers will see him in all his complexity. He was a man who did not want to modernize all of Chinese Buddhism but wished to retain as much traditional Buddhist thought as could be adapted for the modern world. This effort sometimes resulted in awkward juxtapositions and inconsistent recommendations, and it is doubtful that Taixu's program as he conceived it could ever have taken the high ground in China's search for its own version of modernization. Nevertheless, he laid some important groundwork and pointed the way forward, and we shall see in the chapters to come that some later thinkers took up his call to build a Pure Land in the Human Realm with more success. I propose that Taixu is a transitional figure, a midwife who helped a Buddhism that was losing its place in a rapidly evolving world to begin the process of finding its footing. Like Moses, he did not live to enter this new territory himself, but without his vision and initiative, it would have taken far longer for Buddhism to carve out a space for itself and achieve its current degree of popularity.

2

Taixu's Life to 1926

Understanding Taixu's "On the Establishment of the Pure Land in the Human Realm" requires at least a brief look at his life and religious trajectory prior to its composition. A detailed biography is beyond the scope of the present work (see Goodell 2012 for a fuller account of Taixu's life). Here we will give only a general overview, attending particularly to elements of his life and background that help contextualize his Essay. Along the way, we will examine people, events, and influences that had a direct impact on the contents of the Essay in greater depth.

Early Life

Taixu was born on January 8, 1890 as Lü Gansen 呂淦森 to a family with a background in industry and agriculture (Ritzinger 2017, 39). After his father died and his mother remarried, he went to live with his maternal grandmother, a woman who had taken Daoist precepts but whose religious activities were broadly eclectic (Goodell 2012, 18; Jiang 1993, 56). His uncle ran a school that prepared young boys for the imperial examinations, and Taixu studied with him until he was 8 years old. An apt pupil, Taixu quickly mastered his uncle's entire curriculum along with some supplemental materials, and he memorized a great deal of literature (Goodell 2012, 19–20). Between the ages of 9 and 12, he accompanied his grandmother on several trips to famous Buddhist sites (Jiang 1993, 57). These old monasteries, the morning and evening chanting services on the tour boats, the periods of *nianfo* 念佛 (buddha-recollection) practice, as well as the stories of Buddhist and Daoist saints and immortals all left a deep impression on him (Goodell 2012, 20–1).

When he grew older, Taixu's family decided that he needed to focus on earning money and preparing for adult life. He apprenticed at a general store, and while he found the work uninteresting, he was pleased to find that it stocked popular novels that helped him pass the time more pleasantly. His grandmother urged him to continue preparing for the civil service examinations and arranged a prospective bride for him, but Taixu seemed indifferent to a career in retail, government service, the life of a literatus, or marriage. He much preferred his vernacular novels, religious ideas, and travel. He was captivated by exotic tales of Buddhist and Daoist saints, and he dreamed of acquiring supernatural abilities. He loved the antique grandeur of old temples and monasteries, and he conjured fond images of living the life of the monks he saw scuttling about within their walls. Even though he later came to realize that most of what he imagined about temple life was overly romanticized and based on faulty understandings, these images led him to begin thinking seriously about pursuing Buddhist ordination. In 1904, he made his move (Goodell 2012, 23–5).

Ordination and Early Monastic Education

His journey to ordination did not go to plan. He intended to make for Shanghai, but because of various distractions and errors he mistakenly boarded a boat bound for Suzhou during the second leg of his trip. Trying to get back on course, he debarked at Pingwang 平望 and sought lodging at the Xiao Jiuhuashan Monastery 小九華山寺, a place in which he had lodged during earlier pilgrimages with his grandmother. This struck him as fateful, so he decided to seek novice ordination there (Goodell 2012, 26–7). The abbot, Ven. Shida 士達, accepted him; however, because public monasteries such as Xiao Jiuhuashan served the monastic population at large, their resident monks were not permitted to tonsure disciples privately. Therefore, Shida took him to another monastery near Suzhou for tonsure under the master Mingjing 明鏡 (Jiang 1993, 61). Afterward, while training for full ordination, Taixu shuttled between these two monasteries and worked to gain supernatural powers such as invisibility by using practices prescribed by some books he found in them. He did not succeed and was aware of the amusement of the other monks at his efforts (Goodell 2012, 28). He also noticed that many of his fellow monks had joined the monastic order solely to escape military service, and lived dissolute lives of drinking, gambling, and resorting to prostitutes (Jiang 1993, 62). This may well have contributed to his later designs for reform of the monastic order, or *sangha*.

Later that same year, he received the full monastic precepts at the Tiantong Monastery 天童寺 near Ningbo. Several of the monks who officiated at his ordination remained important in Taixu's life and career as friends and mentors.

The main preceptor was Ven. Jichan (寄禪, 1852–1912), also known as "the ascetic Eight Fingers" (*Bazhi Toutuo* 八指頭陀) because he had burned off two of his fingers as an act of devotion. He was an eminent leader of the national Buddhist *sangha*. Liaoyu 了餘, Yuanying (圓瑛, 1878–1953), and Daojie (道階, 1866–1934) also gained prominence later in their careers and played important roles in Taixu's development. According to Jiang Canteng 江燦騰, the intelligence and aptitude for memorizing texts he showed at this time impressed everyone and marked him as a talent to watch (Jiang 1993, 63).

After ordination, Taixu went for a three-year program of study at the Yongfeng Chan Monastery (*Yongfeng chanyuan* 永豊禪院), a temple that trained students to deliver lectures on Buddhist sutras. He also read on his own and meditated (Goodell 2012, 31–2). Eric Goodell reports that during his early years as a monk, Taixu demonstrated such drive and talent that he attracted the attention and support of some of the most high-ranking monks in China (Goodell 2012, 35). Jiang Canteng states that his awareness of his talent made him proud and aloof from other monks (Jiang 1993, 66). In 1907, he went to the Xifang Temple (*Xifang si* 西方寺), also near Ningbo, to read through all the scriptures. He read haphazardly and felt he was making no headway until an unnamed senior monk advised him to read the texts systematically and in order. Upon doing this, he had one of his great religious experiences.

While reading one of the "Perfection of Wisdom" sutras, he suddenly experienced directly the emptiness of all things and his own nonduality with the world around him. At the same time, he had visions of buddha-lands. In one account, he says the state lasted one or two hours, and in another, that it left him with a lasting sense of ease (Goodell 2012, 36–8; Jiang 1993, 70). A few days later, he was reading the *Huayan Sutra* (*Huayan jing* 華嚴經), when he had what he considered the second part of the same experience. As translated by Goodell, he described it in this way:

> After finishing the *Greater Perfection of Wisdom Sūtra*, I began reading the *Huayan jing*. I became aware of the flower store sea of worlds, which I seemed to be personally experiencing. Everything was alive with numinous emptiness. (Goodell 2012, 38)

This experience brought all the abstract teachings in which he had immersed himself to a vivid and harmonious unity, one that deepened his realization but, oddly, deprived him of his ability to memorize texts, as if he had traded in rote memorization for deep understanding (Goodell 2012, 39). This experience solidified his identity as a Buddhist.

Exposure to Socialism and Anarchism

Very soon thereafter, other monks arrived at the Xifang Temple to pursue their own reading programs, but these monks were also conversant in new intellectual and political currents. Among these, Ven. Huashan (華山, 1870–1918) became one of Taixu's best friends, and the two spent long hours discussing new intellectual trends in China (Ritzinger 2017, 40). Taixu, though fascinated, often argued against him from a traditional Buddhist perspective. Nevertheless, in the end, he found Huashan's views compelling, and as he read the books Huashan recommended to him, he became more convinced that Buddhism needed to engage the world to help create a better society (Goodell 2012, 42; Jiang 1993, 81–4). More significantly, several of these books presented utopian visions that later influenced Taixu's Essay. These included Kang Youwei's (康有為, 1858–1927) *Book of the Great Unity* (*Datong shu* 大同書), Tan Sitong's (譚嗣同, 1865–1898) *On Benevolence* (*Renxue* 仁學), and some short works by Zhang Taiyan (章太炎, 1869–1936), among others (Ritzinger 2017, 30–6, 40–1).

He returned to the Xiao Jiuhuashan Monastery where he had been ordained, and there he met the sometime-monk Qiyun (棲雲, d.u.). Like Taixu, he had been ordained under Ven. Jichan, but lived mostly as a layman and resumed his monastic name and robes only when he needed to take shelter in a Buddhist temple (Ritzinger 2017, 41). Qiyun had studied in Japan and become part of Sun Yat-sen's revolutionary movement, and his influence moved Taixu even further into radical politics (Ritzinger 2017, 41; Jiang 1993, 84–5). According to Justin Ritzinger, it was at this point that Taixu committed to anarchism, which at the time seemed like an awakening, but which Taixu later understood as a "fall from grace" or a "return to the dusts of the world" (Ritzinger 2017, 41).

Taixu's activities over the next couple of years were driven by two things: the appearance of Japanese Buddhist missionaries in China and the Qing government's moves to confiscate Buddhist temple properties and convert them for new uses. The Japanese claimed that Chinese Buddhism was backward and corrupt, and represented Japanese Buddhist teachings as more suited to modern social needs. The Qing government claimed that Buddhist clergy contributed nothing of value to society and that their buildings could economically house modern schools that would train students to deal with emerging social needs. The clergy fought back in various ways, which have been documented in several scholarly studies (e.g., Goossaert 2006; Nedostup 2009, 39–43). In some quarters, monastic counterproposals addressed the

Japanese missionary and Qing policy challenges simultaneously as temples worked with Japanese missionaries to establish schools in their monasteries and to join Japanese Buddhist organizations as branch temples (Jiang 1993, 89–90). The first move countered the government's rationale for confiscating temple property, and the second gave Chinese Buddhists some protection by ceding control of their properties to organizations with extraterritorial privileges (Goodell 2012, 46–7).

In 1908, Taixu, Huashan, and Qiyun joined forces with other members of the clergy under the leadership of his mentor Jichan to form the Sangha Education Association (*Seng[jia] jiaoyu hui* 僧[伽]教育會; Ritzinger 2017, 41). The purpose was to work with the Qing government rather than with Japanese Buddhist groups to avert temple property confiscations. In 1910, they established the Sangha Normal School (*Seng shifan xuetang* 僧師範學堂) in Nanjing, whose mission was to train monastics in secular subjects so that they could staff the planned temple-schools, again preempting the government's rationale for confiscation (Goodell 2012, 50). Taixu himself went to Nanjing in 1909 to attend classes for one term at the Jetavana Hermitage (*Zhihuan jingshe* 祇洹精舍), where for a brief period he experienced Buddhist "new education" firsthand. This meant that in addition to traditional Buddhist topics, he studied Japanese and English as well as other subjects deemed conducive to China's forward development.

Taixu and Qiyun went to Guangzhou in early 1910 to help set up a branch of the Sangha Education Association at the Shuangxi Temple (*Shuangxi si* 雙溪寺) and began giving lectures and publishing some of his earliest works. Soon after he arrived, the abbot of the Shuangxi Temple retired and Taixu assumed the office (Ritzinger 2017, 42). At the same time, he began secretly attending socialist and anarchist meetings, which he found exciting and a bit frightening given the unruliness of many of the participants (Goodell 2012, 53, 57; Ritzinger 2017, 42). In the spring of 1911, several of his associates were involved in an uprising against the Qing government that failed, and in the aftermath a poem he had written praising those who had died in the rebellion surfaced, prompting the authorities to seek his arrest. They surrounded his monastery, but he was in a newspaper office in the city at the time and evaded capture. Some influential friends interceded on his behalf and the charges were dropped, but he was still ordered to leave Guangzhou (Goodell 2012, 57, 58; Jiang 1993, 96). He returned to Shanghai, where he continued his study of anarchism and socialism.

The "Invasion of Jinshan"

Sun Yat-sen's uprising toppled the Qing dynasty later the same year, succeeding where Taixu's associates in Guangzhou had failed, and the new Republic of China was proclaimed on January 1, 1912. Taixu went to Nanjing, the seat of the new government, and stayed in the Pilu Monastery (*Pilu si* 比盧寺), then a center of socialist thought (Goodell 2012, 63). The Chinese Socialist Party came into being at this time, quickly swelling in numbers but without articulating a shared ideology that all members could embrace. The Pilu Monastery served as its Nanjing headquarters, and Taixu joined and became one of its leaders (Ritzinger 2017, 46–7). In Nanjing, Taixu made favorable contacts with members of the new government, and with their encouragement he worked on a charter for a proposed Buddhist organization to be called the "Association for the Advancement of Buddhism" (*Fojiao xiejin hui* 佛教協進會). His efforts to hold an organizing meeting at the famous Jinshan Monastery (*Jinshan si* 金山寺), however, lurched unexpectedly off course, leading to the incident known in English as the "Invasion of Jinshan" and in Chinese as the "great disturbance at Jinshan" (*da nao Jinshan* 大鬧金山). This event altered the subsequent course of Taixu's career, and it unfolded as follows.

When Taixu arrived in Nanjing, he found that one of his former fellow students from the Jetavana Hermitage, Ven. Renshan (仁山, 1887–1951) was already there. They worked together to formulate a plan for setting up the new association, and Renshan obtained permission to hold the organizational meeting at the Jinshan Monastery, the place where he first entered the *sangha*. Many local Buddhist clergy came, but Taixu and Renshan also invited many of their socialist and anarchist associates from nearby Zhenjiang 鎮江 to attend. Participants numbered between three hundred and four hundred (Jiang 1993, 102).

Taixu called the meeting for the sole stated purpose of presenting his proposal and charter for the new association. During the meeting, however, Renshan got up and proposed taking over the Jinshan monastic complex and making it the headquarters for the association, and furthermore to use the rest of its facilities for a modern-style school. When one of the resident monastic officials spoke out sharply against such a takeover, he was shouted down and physically assaulted by Renshan's sympathizers, leading him and others of his faction to leave. Thinking they had won, Renshan and his followers began surveying the monastery's buildings and grounds the following day to decide on the placement of the various association and school offices and classrooms. However, the resident faction went to court to stop the takeover and, with the help of some armed locals, returned and drove Taixu, Renshan, and their sympathizers out. What had begun as a simple organizational meeting to ratify a charter had devolved into a failed *putsch* very quickly.

Sealed Confinement

Taixu's reputation was ruined and he was adrift. Newspapers largely blamed him for the debacle, and later in his life he reflected that the incident made him a "revolutionary Buddhist" in the eyes of the public (quoted in Goodell 2012, 68–9). At the same time, several changes in China and the world shook his faith in his previous path. These included Yuan Shikai's accession to the presidency and the new religious policies he put in place, Yuan's proscription of the Socialist Party after 1913, the fact that the fall of the Qing had loosened government oversight of Buddhism and opened a way for the laity to organize independently of the clergy, and the loss of confidence that Western political ideas could help China following the outbreak of the First World War. All of these developments led Taixu to believe that he needed to take some time to retrench. So, after a couple of years helping his mentor Jichan with a nationwide Buddhist association and editing a Buddhist journal, he returned to Mount Putuo in early 1914 to arrange for a three-year period of sealed confinement (*biguan* 閉關). This was a venerable monastic practice in which, with great ritual fanfare at both the beginning and the end, a monk was sealed in a small hut for three years during which, freed from the usual round of temple responsibilities, he could focus on study, meditation, and renewal.

He arrived in the spring of 1914 to arrange for a room and support services at Mount Putuo. As Jiang Canteng notes, one of the reasons he chose Mount Putuo as the site for his sealed confinement was that in 1909, when he taught there for half a year, and in 1911, when he fled there, he had known Yinguang 印光. The two men were friendly, talked for long hours, exchanged poems, and Yinguang thought highly of Taixu. Mount Putuo was the site where Yinguang underwent his own period of confinement, so Taixu followed suit. In his autobiography, he reported the following:

> Aside from sometimes visiting with Ven. Yushan and Ven. Zhiyuan, I could also enjoy the company of Ven. Huoxuan or visit Ven. Yinguang at the Scripture Pavilion in the rear temple, often passing the entire day in pleasant conversation

with him, calm in body and mind. I also heard Ven. Liaoyu talk about years past (while we were in the room in which I was to pass my period of sealed confinement) when he practiced the *nianfo samādhi* and had a period of personal realization of the nature of mind. I composed a poem to commemorate this, and it helped to fix my resolve on doing my sealed confinement at Mount Putuo. (quoted in Jiang 1993, 126; see also Goodell 2012, 75)[1]

Yinguang himself applied the seal to the doors when the period of confinement began in August.

I wish to draw particular attention to this connection with Yinguang. Modern Chinese Buddhist histories often portray Taixu and Yinguang as two of the four great monks of the early Republican period. As noted in the introduction, the four represented the reinvigoration of different aspects of Buddhist life, which implies that each figure had an exclusive connection with one area of endeavor. In particular, if Taixu is the modernizer and Yinguang is the Pure Land conservative, then it is easy to frame them as ideological opposites. As we will see in the next chapter, modern scholars who view Taixu purely as a modernizer who opposed traditional Pure Land practice cast him as Yinguang's natural adversary. However, the two knew each other, had friendly conversations, and put forward ideas on traditional Pure Land themes. The translation of Taixu's Essay that follows (Chapter 6) will demonstrate this clearly.

During his three years of confinement, Taixu kept to a strict schedule of meditation, study, and writing. He had two profound religious experiences, and wrote two important works, one on reformation of the Buddhist monastic system and the other a *summa* of Buddhist teachings and their relation to the welfare of the nation and the world. The religious experiences, he reports, enhanced his understanding of Buddhist scriptures and the meaning of mind-only philosophy (*weixin sixiang* 唯心思想), and Eric Goodell surmises that they influenced his writings, especially the guidebook to Buddhism (Goodell 2012, 94, 95). However, for purposes of understanding the Essay, the *Proposal for Institutional Reform in the Sangha* (*Zhengli sengqie zhidu lun* 整理僧伽制度論) may be more salient (see Goodell 2012, 98–105, for an extensive summary of this text). In it, we find a definition of the Pure Land School, his classification of the traditional eight schools of Buddhism (*ba zong* 八宗) as he interpreted them, and a plan for a centralized training monastery for the entire *sangha*.

---

[1] Many thanks to Eric Goodell for pointers on the English translation in e-mails dated September 22, 2019.

Taixu understood Chinese Buddhism to have branched into eight individual schools, which he named as follows:

1. The Qingliang School (*qingliang zong* 清涼宗), or Huayan School (*huayan zong* 華嚴宗);
2. The Tiantai School (*tiantai zong* 天台宗), or Dharma-Lotus School (*fahua zong* 法華宗);
3. The Jiaxiang School (*jiaxiang zong* 嘉祥宗), or Sanlun School (*sanlun zong* 三論宗);
4. The Ci'en School (*ci'en zong* 慈恩宗), or Consciousness-only School (*weishi zong* 唯識宗);
5. The Lushan School (*lushan zong* 廬山宗), or Pure Land School (*jingtu zong* 淨土宗);
6. The Kaiyuan School (*kaiyuan zong* 開元宗), or Mantra School (*zhenyan zong* 真言宗);
7. The Shaoshi School (*shaoshi zong* 少室宗), or Chan School (*chan zong* 禪宗); and
8. The Southern Mountain School (*nanshan zong* 南山宗), or Vinaya School (*lü zong* 律宗). (Taixu 1915, n.p.)

The way Taixu explains these schools will help put certain aspects of the Essay into their proper framework. First, the organization of Chinese Buddhism into these eight schools will determine the key features of the Buddhist utopian community that he envisioned in the Essay. As we will see, the compound was to feature halls dedicated to the teachings and practice of each school. Second, Taixu's understanding of the Pure Land School undergirds the entire Essay. In this *Proposal*, Taixu describes the Pure Land School as follows:

> The Lushan School, formerly known as the "Pure Land School" or the "Lotus School" (*lian zong* 蓮宗): There are two meanings of "Pure Land" or "Lotus." One is overly broad, indicating all the Pure Lands that lie beyond this world in the ten directions. Whether in the Lotus-Treasury world or in the Sahā world (i.e., the present defiled world), nothing lies outside of this great lotus blossom. The other meaning is too narrow, [covering nothing but] Amitābha's Land of Utmost Bliss. That which is pure is not limited to [the buddhas'] fields, nor is it limited to [one on the] lotus-thrones. Nowadays this school is given a set name according to the first patriarch recognized from ancient times until the present (i.e., Lushan Huiyuan). [Other] patriarchs have extended its glory, its practices and doctrines are well set, it is outstanding and there is nothing to change in it. (Taixu 1915, n.p.)

The last few sentences explain why Taixu thought one should call this School the "Lushan School": the first "patriarch" was Lushan Huiyuan (廬山慧遠, 334–416 CE), and the Chinese Pure Land tradition has held that a line of succeeding patriarchs carry it forward into the present (Jones 2019, ch. 8 and appendix). His dismissal of definitions of this school, which he considered as "overly broad" or "too narrow," is also reflected in the Essay. He certainly rejects the idea that the Pure Land embraces all of reality, whether pure or impure, since everything is part of the "lotus blossom world." If that were true, then there would be no rationale for a distinctive Pure Land School at all. On the other hand, the fact that he does not want it understood narrowly as devotion to the Buddha Amitābha and practices aimed at gaining rebirth only in his land—Sukhāvatī—helps us understand why the Essay talks about rebirth either in that Pure Land or in the Inner Court of Maitreya as equally valid aspirations. He thus defended the latter goal's legitimacy against a tradition that for centuries had denigrated it as inferior. He wanted the Pure Land School, understood in this way, to have a continuing institutional presence within a reformed *sangha* and in his ideal community.

Return to the World

Taixu emerged from his hut in the spring of 1917 and found that both he and the world had changed. From this point onward, he refrained from overt political activism and focused his attention on the reform of Chinese Buddhism. Yuan Shikai, the president who tried to become a new emperor, had died and China had fallen into disunity as warlords took control of large swaths of territory. The proposed law for regulating Buddhism that provided the impetus for his *Proposal* fell by the wayside, and Buddhism was left to its own devices. In the years that followed, many thinkers came forward with plans for China's uplift, and in many instances these planners believed that religion was an impediment to progress and gave it no positive role in their schemes. At the same time, another segment of the educated classes developed a fascination with Tantric Buddhist magic and ritual (Tarocco 2007, 39–41). In response to these developments, Taixu shifted his focus to clergy education and reform and engaged with the emerging urban culture.

After three years in a confined space, Taixu decided to travel to various Buddhist sites and reacquaint himself with the religious landscape. On one of his trips, he renewed contact with Ven. Yuanying, who asked him to go to Taiwan on his behalf in response to an invitation that he had had to decline. Taixu accepted, and through this journey deepened his knowledge of and connection to Japanese Buddhism, since Taiwan at that time was part of Japan (Goodell 2012, 109, 110; Jones 1999, chs. 2, 3).

First Trip to Japan

Through Ven. Shanhui (善慧, 1881–1945), his connection in Taiwan, Taixu was able to arrange a trip to Japan immediately (on Shanhui, see Jones 1999, 39–44). Taixu had wanted to go to Japan for some time, and the trip to Taiwan offered him a stepping-stone. To him, Japanese Buddhism seemed organized in ways that resembled his vision for Chinese Buddhism save that it lacked a nationwide Buddhist organization at its apex. He appreciated the advances Japanese Buddhist scholars had made in the study of Buddhist texts and history, and he admired their educational system and Buddhist universities, upon whose curricula he took careful notes (Jiang 1993, 147–8; Goodell 2012, 116–18). He was very interested in the missionaries that various schools of Japanese Buddhism had sent abroad, and later he would incorporate such missions into his plans for an ideal Buddhist community in the Essay (Goodell 2012, 114). He found that the sectarian structure of Japanese Buddhism tallied well with his own desire to organize Chinese Buddhism along the lines of the traditional eight schools. The Japanese model showed how such disparate schools could be ordered in such a way that they kept their individual identities while collaborating in common pursuits (Goodell 2012, 115). All in all, he found the visit to Japan stimulating for his own reform plans, although he did not wish to emulate the Japanese clergy's adoption of clerical marriage and acceptance of meat and alcohol consumption (Goodell 2012, 119).

The Bodhi Society and *Haichaoyin*

When he arrived back in China in late 1917, Taixu returned to Mount Putuo with the intention of pursuing his reform activities, but things did not go smoothly. Right then, several members of the Uniform Virtue Society (*Tongshan she* 同善社), a "redemption society," paid him a visit. After speaking with Taixu, some of them converted to Buddhism and immediately began planning a new, Buddhist-based association that took shape as the Bodhi Society (*Jue she* 覺社). Several of its first recruits were highly placed members of society who had the means to provide financial support for various activities, such as publishing some of Taixu's early works. The society set up shop in Shanghai, and it planned to offer a regular series of lectures, which fit well with Taixu's dream of launching centers for lay education as part of his overall plan for *sangha* reform (Goodell 2012, 123). Eventually, the Bodhi Society hoped to have branches in several major cities. Early signatories to the society included Liu Renhang (劉仁航, 1884–1938), whose own writing and activities informed portions of Taixu's Essay, as we shall see in Chapter 4 (Jiang 1993, 151).

Another of the Bodhi Society's stated purposes was to foster the publication of Buddhist books and magazines (Jiang 1993, 149). The society's quarterly journal provided a venue for the works Taixu had composed while in sealed confinement, but the most significant development came after 1919. In response to the May Fourth and New Culture movements, Taixu moved the magazine's place of publication in 1920 and changed it to a monthly called *Haichaoyin* (海潮音, *Sound of the Ocean Tide*; see Jiang 1993, 152). While the Bodhi Society eventually became inactive, this magazine has been published continuously to the present day and is one of the most widely read Buddhist reviews in China. Goodell believes the society declined largely because Taixu stopped promoting it, preferring to work on the magazine instead. The society appealed to an old guard increasingly seen as reactionary, while the magazine attained nationwide reach and spoke to members of a newly emergent urban middle class (Goodell 2012, 132–3).

Editing this magazine not only gave Taixu an outlet for his own writings, but exposed him to the ideas of other Buddhist thinkers, one of whom seems to have influenced his thoughts about modernizing Pure Land. In June 1924, the magazine published an article on "establishing a new Pure Land" (*Jianshe xin jingtu* 建設新淨土) by Tang Dayuan (唐大圓, 1890?–1941). Tang's description of his "new Pure Land" bore a striking resemblance to the concept of the Pure Land in the Human Realm that Taixu would propose two years later, and Taixu must have found the idea intriguing. He not only published the article but provided a short preface for it. We will rely on Jakub Zamorski's recent study for a summary of Tang's proposals (Zamorski 2019).

Tang had originally followed the Pure Land traditionalist Yinguang, but by the 1920s his ideas began to turn toward questions of fitting Pure Land belief and practice to the needs of the modern world (Zamorski 2019, 106–7). He came to believe that the practices of *nianfo* (as oral recitation of or mental contemplation of the Buddha Amitābha's name) and devotion to Amitābha should be primarily for the purpose of benefitting other beings. While he never stopped believing that *nianfo* would bring the practitioner to the Pure Land after death, he also began to teach that the practice also helped purify the mind, and, as the *Vimalakīrti Sūtra* stated, when the mind is pure, the land becomes pure. Thus, the purity of mind that resulted from the practice of traditional *nianfo* would simultaneously work to turn this world into a pure land, to the benefit of both self and others (Zamorski 2019, 107). In addition, he organized like-minded believers into societies for the joint practice of *nianfo* so that their individual practice would, through the mechanism of sympathetic resonance (*ganying* 感應), allow each practitioner to enjoy the benefit of everyone's practice, thus maximizing the purifying effect.

In his *Haichaoyin* article, Tang declared that the individual's mind and body form an appropriate basis for founding the "new Pure Land," but practitioners needed to take other steps to extend the benefit beyond their own salvation. They needed to spread the good word and set an example for their fellow human beings in order to make virtue flourish. If they could get others to practice *nianfo*, then the synergy of sympathetic resonance would magnify the purifying effect of the practice across society (Zamorski 2019, 111–14). He contrasted this with socialist schemes, such as the Kropotkin-inspired New Villages, that had been tried in China and found wanting. For Tang, their lack of a spiritual base prevented them from providing peace and serenity. Focus on the Pure Land could bring these about with ease since, in his theory, such efforts at social uplift would be reinforced by the other-power of Amitābha (Zamorski 2019, 115).

We see in Tang's proposal the following elements: (1) that practitioners of Pure Land should not neglect the present world and society; (2) that traditional aspirations for rebirth in the Pure Land are perfectly compatible with the desire to benefit other beings in the present; (3) that the practice of *nianfo*, by purifying the individual's mind and body, also purifies the world; (4) that when many people covenant to practice *nianfo* together, their individual efforts resonate and amplify the purifying effects into the world around them; and (5) that when these effects reach a critical mass, then the Pure Land appears not just in a future rebirth, but here and now. These ideas are not identical to Taixu's (e.g., Taixu did not teach that Amitābha's other-power would directly empower human efforts at social reform), and Zamorski reports that later in life Tang abandoned them and adopted Taixu's vision shortly after Taixu published his Essay (Zamorski 2019, 120). We cannot know the extent to which Tang Dayuan's article influenced Taixu's reflections on the Pure Land in the Human Realm, but later, Tang's ideas would resurface in Taiwan in the pages of the magazine *Buddhist Culture*, as we will see in Chapter 7.

Other Influences

According to Taixu's own report, he drew more direct inspiration for the Essay from sources other than Tang Dayuan's article on the "new pure land." When the Essay appeared in *Haichaoyin* in 1926, he prefaced it with a brief paragraph detailing some conversations he had engaged in with his associates.

> The circumstances that led to this Essay go back ten years when I was with Liu Renhang trying to build his Requiting Kindness Village (*Bao'en Cun* 報恩村). Over the years [I have] encountered military and business leaders; they were fearful of the impending calamity of "going red" (*chihua* 赤化). They were particularly worried about a crisis of life and property. The layman Sun Houzai (孫厚在) repeatedly said ordinary peoples' livelihoods are constrained, economic revolution was unavoidable, and the old Buddhist monastic system would have to gradually change so that clergy earn their living doing agriculture and forestry in the countryside. If they didn't they would have a hard time surviving. (Taixu 1956, 349)

Several of the concerns that Taixu takes up early in the Essay appear here. He had been spending time in a utopian experimental village run by Liu Renhang, who we met earlier as a charter member of the Bodhi Society. His contacts were telling him that threats to "life and property" kept them preoccupied, and they worried about a vaguely defined threat that political parties will "go red."[2] Taixu will address these concerns directly in these terms in the first few pages of his Essay.

He goes on to say that his primary motivation for composing the Essay came from a pair of letters he received from another lay follower named Zang Guanchan (藏貫禪), which he reproduced in full as a preface to the Essay.

In these letters, Zang echoes Taixu's other interlocutors in boiling all of humanity's problems down to the twin desires for life and property. These desires have led to conflict and mass slaughter at every level of society from

---

[2] This term was not clearly defined in public political discourse. People such as those Taixu spoke with tossed about the term "going red," along with its opposite "anti-red" (*fanchi* 反赤), usually with an implication of extremism, as needed to make their points. I will explore this in more depth in notes attached to the translation. See Wang Jianwei 2010.

the personal to the familial to the global. As a remedy, Zang asks Taixu to devote his organizational talent to the founding of a worldwide Buddhist association that would have branches in several different countries. Members of this organization would donate all of their private property to it and settle into Buddhist communities, within which each would receive what they needed to maintain an appropriate standard of living. Significantly, Zang says that the result of this plan would be to bring about a "magnificent Pure Land in this present world" (*jianli xianshi zhuangyan jingtu* 建立現世莊嚴淨土). He repeats this in the second letter, using the terms "new Pure Land" (*xin jingtu* 新淨土) or "new worldwide Pure Land" (*shijie xin jingtu* 世界新淨土).

In these letters, Zang offers many details about his projected organization's structure and financing, internal discipline, and relations with host countries, but these are sketchy and muddled and need not detain us here. What should attract our notice is that Taixu credited these letters with motivating him to compose the Essay, and within the Essay he refers back to the second letter and suggests that some unspecified aspects of Zang's plan might work. The following features of Zang's letters also guide Taixu's thought: the need for Buddhist solutions to accord with modern trends; the centrality of grasping at life and property in the genesis of current conflicts; the need for a Buddhist association and the establishment of ideal Buddhist communities; the need for cooperation with local governments; and the use of a term analogous to Taixu's "Pure Land in the Human Realm" to describe the final result. Like Tang Dayuan's term "new Pure Land," Zang's phrases "new Pure Land" and "worldwide new Pure Land" seem to have implanted the idea in Taixu's mind that a reconfiguration of the concept of the Pure Land that would bring it down to earth might provide a good slogan for the promotion of Buddhist solutions to current problems. As we shall see, however, his use of another term, "Pure Land in the Human Realm," broadened the referent beyond what either Tang or Zang envisioned. Nevertheless, Taixu appears to have built on ideas that were in the air when developing this concept, and one may well wonder whether or not he would have come up with the "Pure Land in the Human Realm" without these influences.

Lecture Activities

At this time, Taixu also began giving lectures on Buddhist texts, not in temples as had been the custom previously, but in urban halls where he spoke primarily to lay audiences for reasons, as we will explain in the next section (Goodell 2012,

126). As we will see in Chapter 3, this is where many Western interlocutors first met him and were surprised to see the ritualized nature of these lectures, which manifested in chanting and periods of *nianfo* before a statue of Amitābha. They presumed that Taixu did this only to please the crowds, but the main argument of this book is that Taixu sincerely wanted to incorporate traditional elements into these events. In his writings, he also took a moderate political position compared to his earlier revolutionary stance, one that embraced both social reform and Buddhism as essential to forward progress. This placed him in between radical secular reformers and religious conservatives, though his writings at the time suggest he leaned somewhat to the conservative side of the median. For example, he continued to defend the notion that one could gain supernatural powers (*shentong* 神通) through Buddhist cultivation (Goodell 2012, 138).

In 1921, Taixu was invited to assume the abbacy of the Jingci Temple 淨慈寺 in Hangzhou, and while his tenure lasted only about a year before he was forced out, two facets of his administration bear on the Essay. First, he implemented several provisions of his monastic reform program by regularizing and updating monastic offices and tightening discipline for the resident clergy. Second, he prescribed new rites for morning and evening devotional services and for daily periods of meditation. Notably, he renamed the meditation hall the "Hall of the Horned Tiger," a reference to a verse attributed to Yongming Yanshou (永明延壽, 904–975 CE) which declared that one who practices both Chan and Pure Land is like a tiger with horns, that is, doubly capable (Jones 2019, 120). He implemented periods of *nianfo* as part of the practice, which again casts doubt on the claim that any interest he showed toward Pure Land teaching and practice was a mere expedient and not an authentic expression of his own commitments (Goodell 2012, 158–61). A protracted lawsuit led to his ouster by the provincial governor, and he ceded his abbacy in May 1922.

The fourth chapter of Eric Goodell's dissertation describes changes in society and education that led Taixu to reconfigure his teaching for a new audience. The "old model" positioned Buddhist temples as sites of pilgrimage and Buddhist clergy as leaders supported by local gentry educated in traditional Confucian academies. It presumed the social hierarchy of the late empire and a premodern cosmology in which services rendered to gods and ancestors figured prominently. However, with the abrogation of the civil examination system in 1905, its replacement by a secular education system, and the rapid influx of global learning, this old system became increasingly untenable. Taixu saw the signs clearly during the 1920s and began adjusting his reform program in several ways. His writing style became less classical and more vernacular; he calibrated his message for people educated in the new system, which meant removing service to deities and traditional merit-making activities in favor of work toward more tangible goals; and he moved from traditional temple settings to urban lecture halls. Through these and other ways, he shifted his focus from the "retired gentleman," who could take long retreats away from his duties for periods of personal cultivation, to the urban citizen who needed to go to work every day and remain at home with his family. Put more succinctly, his target audience changed from the gentry class to the middle class (Goodell 2012, 172–4).

It would be a mistake to think that he intended to completely secularize Buddhism, as several modern scholars have presumed. Instead, he still aimed at moving his audience toward Mahayana Buddhist goals such as rebirth in the Pure Land and buddhahood. What changed was the starting point. Now he wanted to communicate with a modern public in terms they could relate to and move from there to the perennial objectives of Buddhist practice. He found help in some useful terminology in a debate that began in 1923 around the issue of science and religion. On one side were intellectuals who believed that science could bring society an adequate blueprint for a viable way of life unsupplemented by any religious elements at all, while on the other, there were those who insisted that religion still had a role to play. The term adopted for the object of the debate was "philosophy of human life" (*rensheng guan* 人生觀), and Taixu later adopted the phrase "human life," a term not previously prominent in Buddhist literature, as a way to summarize the new direction he projected for Buddhism.

Taixu put forward his thoughts in his 1924 essay "Humanistic Science" (*Renshengguan de kexue* 人生觀的科學; summarized in Goodell 2012, 185–96). This piece is long and complex, so here I will confine my presentation only to the parts that bear on his later Essay. In contrast to the wider debate, which pitted science against Confucianism and Western intuitionism, he staked out a position centered on Buddhism. He claimed that in Buddhism the goals and methods of both religion and science converge as Buddhist techniques of self-cultivation call practitioners to observe their own mental states empirically and proceed according to actual experiences and results. When carried to its fullest extent, he claimed it would lead to the attainment of a buddha's omniscience. Its yogic methods made Buddhism a higher kind of science (Goodell 2012, 190–1).

Scholars are in agreement that one of the most important consequences of Taixu's remapping of the path from human being to buddha is that it bypassed all intermediate goals (such as becoming an *arhat* or a *pratyekabuddha*) and intermediaries (*devas* and other spirit-beings as well as his dismissal of

Christianity and local spirit cults). Instead, he "directly linked" (*zhijie* 直接) humans to buddhas (Goodell 2012, 187; Hong 1999, 137–8). This reconfiguration of Buddhist goals was not a mere doctrinal adjustment. It pointed practitioners away from periods of secluded practice removed from the hurly-burly of daily life (which favored the old gentry class) and toward a model of active engagement in society, a formulation more favorable to the urban middle class. If one could become a buddha from the midst of "human life," then immersion in human life mattered more than involvement with spiritual beings. Keeping this in mind will help the reader better understand Taixu's efforts to connect compassionate work in the world ("human life") with the aim of rebirth in a buddha-land. The latter was a traditional way of taking practitioners at the moment of death directly from their human rebirth to a place where, *as humans*, they could move toward the attainment of buddhahood with no intermediary helpers or stages.

Taixu boiled all this down to a single term in 1927 or 1928[3] when he began to refer to his teaching as "Buddhism for Human Life" (*rensheng fojiao* 人生佛教). The term "Pure Land in the Human Realm" that appears in the 1926 Essay thus predates this term, and we should regard the Essay as a precursor, not a derivative, of this formula (Goodell 2012, 168–9, 203). The intent of the Essay becomes more legible if one bears this in mind while reading it, as it lays out a program for improving life in the present while claiming that doing so is not incompatible with very traditional Buddhist goals.

Finally, it is interesting that in this 1924 work he proposed a simple agrarian and communal life as the most conducive to the attainment of buddhahood. In this scheme, clergy and laity would dwell together in a rustic mountainside community and work together, echoing the tales of Buddhist sages of old such as Baizhang 百丈 and Pang Yun 龐蘊 (Goodell 2012, 195). We will see this idea articulated again in the Essay when he describes the establishment of such a community as one possible way to actualize the Pure Land in the Human Realm.

World Buddhist Federation and the Great East Asian Buddhist Conference

One of the oddest episodes in Taixu's life concerns the establishment of the "World Buddhist Federation" (*Shijie fojiao lianhehui* 世界佛教聯合會) and its subsequent participation in the 1925 Great East Asian Buddhist Conference

---

[3] Hong Jinlian 洪金蓮 gives the date as Year of the Republic 17 (民 17; see Hong 1999, 137–8).

(*Dongya fojiao dahui* 東亞佛教大會) in Japan. In 1923, many Christian missionary operations had encroached on Mount Lu (*Lushan* 廬山), a place of great significance in Chinese Buddhist history. It was the abode of the first patriarch of the Pure Land School, for which reason Taixu gave it the alternative name Lushan School as seen above. Taixu arranged with the Dalin Temple (*Dalin si* 大林寺) to use one of its halls for a summer lecture series and office space (Jiang 1993, 187), and in that place Taixu had a few of his dialogues with Western Christians and scholars such as Frank Millican and Clarence Hamilton (see next chapter). Yan Shaofu 嚴少孚, who was responsible for arranging the living quarters, took it upon himself to hang a sign outside with "World Buddhist Federation" written upon it (Jiang 1993, 188).

When Taixu arrived, he noticed the sign but did not order it removed even though no such organization existed, and so it remained in place for Buddhist pilgrims and assorted vacationers to see. One of these was a professor from Ōtani University in Japan named Inada Ensai 稻田圓成, who had come to Mount Lu specifically to meet Taixu. The two discussed ways that Chinese and Japanese Buddhists could work together, and Inada saw this fictitious organization as a possible platform for cooperation (Jiang 1993, 190; Yinshun 2000, 160–1). Inada said that Buddhism presented an avenue for China and Japan to overcome the barriers that had arisen between them and proposed student exchanges and joint intellectual activities. Although Taixu was cool to the idea of exchanging students, he saw possibilities in pursuing this relationship. Hence, in the following year (1924), the Japanese sent a delegation to Mount Lu to join in the planning sessions for the World Buddhist Federation (Jiang 1993, 191; Yinshun 2000, 161). This prompted Taixu to make a formal application to the Chinese government to approve the charter for this new organization.

Once he had the approval in hand, Taixu began inviting Buddhists from other parts of Asia to Mount Lu to participate in the lecture series, but from the beginning only China and Japan played active roles. A few Western Buddhists gave talks only because they already happened to be in Mount Lu, but no one came from elsewhere in response to Taixu's invitations (Jiang 1993, 196). In light of this, Taixu agreed to a suggestion from the Japanese that the name be changed to "East Asian Buddhist Federation" (*Dongya fojiao lianhehui* 東亞佛教聯合會), though he hoped the organization would not relinquish its global aspirations (Jiang 1993, 199). Taixu further agreed to establish a "Chinese Buddhist Federation" (*Zhonghua fojiao lianhehui* 中華佛教聯合會), whose participation in the East Asian organization would give the latter a true multinational membership, and he agreed to lead a delegation from this new federation to a conference in Japan in 1925.

Thus, in October 1925, Taixu led a group of twenty-six Chinese monks and laymen to Japan for the "Great East Asian Buddhist Conference." Jiang Canteng reports that Taixu was everywhere, giving thirty speeches and networking actively. *The Young East* published an English translation of one of his speeches the same year under the title "A Statement to Asiatic Buddhists" (Taixu 1925)—a text that advances several of the themes that dominate his Essay: namely, the turmoil caused by modern warfare, class struggle and the exploitation of workers, natural calamities that uproot lives, and so on. He says that on the surface, imperialism and capitalism seem to be behind all this suffering, but in fact it is Western civilization's loss of its spiritual moorings and drift toward materialism that are to blame. With spiritual constraints gone, nations wage wars of conquest upon each other, families disintegrate, the wealth gap grows ever larger, and no one knows any peace. So far socialism and anarchism have failed to provide remedies because, lacking a basis in spiritual cultivation, their proponents are driven by deep-rooted greed and ignorance just as much as the colonialists and oppressors. Western monotheism has been equally unavailing as the advance of science has eroded its credibility. Taixu concludes that only Buddhism, which accords with science and provides the means for spiritual uplift, can address the world's current problems.

However, Buddhists have not roused themselves to assist in solving contemporary problems, and Taixu enumerates four reasons for this failure:

> First, they are seldom interested in social service or the work of educating the society. The priests or rather monks are generally ignorant and their services to society are confined to singing of masses and prayers in the funeral services. Secondly, although the monks divide themselves into sects or schools, each pursuing a special object, yet they always fail to accomplish that object. Thirdly, the monks are always religious recluses, taking no interest in the affairs of the community or the country and they are in turn slighted by the Government or the ruling classes. Fourthly, most of the Chinese Buddhist monks lack the necessary modern scientific knowledge and are also ignorant of the current thoughts and ideas in the world. (Taixu 1925, 179)

He goes on to catalog the strengths and weaknesses of Chinese and Japanese Buddhists, and recommends that they cooperate and learn from one another in order to bring help to a suffering world. Significantly for our understanding the Essay, which would appear the following year, he states that Buddhists should engage not only in concrete social work (famine relief, promotion of industry, infrastructure development, and so on) but also in offering services and practicing *nianfo* (or "muttering of prayers and names of the Buddha etc. etc."; see Taixu 1925, 181).

Also significant for the Essay is the fact that one Liu Renxuan 劉仁宣 went as part of the delegation (Jiang 1993, 210). He was a close relative of Liu Renhang 劉仁航, whom we have met several times now in various connections. He was the author of a compilation of excerpts from Chinese utopian literature called *Case Studies of Datong in the East* (*Dongfang datong xue'an* 東方大同學案), which was slated for publication in 1926, the same year that Taixu's Essay appeared. According to the preface Taixu provided for this work, Liu Renxuan brought an outline of this book to Japan, where Taixu looked it over (Liu 2014 [1926], 1:1–2). As we will see in Chapter 4, this work provided the basis for some of the Essay's contents.

Return from Japan

Taixu returned from Japan in November 1925, and though he had met many delegates from Sri Lanka and Korea, nothing further came of the Great East Asian Buddhist Conference. Taixu never visited Japan again, and Japan had increasing difficulty gaining access to Chinese Buddhist temples on the mainland as hostilities between warlords in the north made it difficult to travel (Jiang 1993, 215). Meanwhile, many of Taixu's other reform efforts were faltering. His seminaries were closing, a Buddhist youth organization that he had established slipped from his control, and he still had adversarial relations with the conservative monastic faction. As Jiang Canteng points out, it was time for his program to enter a new phase (Jiang 1993, 215).

Summary and Conclusion

It was at this particular juncture that Taixu composed his Essay, and so it is worth pausing for a moment to take stock of everything that had happened with Taixu and China up to this time. Taixu had spent his youth immersed in very traditional Buddhist beliefs and practices, and he was deeply involved in anarchist study and action. He brought the zeal of his new friends and ideas to his initial reform efforts with disastrous results. The "Invasion of Jinshan" had alienated him from the conservative monks who had once been his mentors, and he was still too young to have the standing needed to initiate a movement of his own. He went into a three-year period of seclusion in which he both expanded his knowledge and deepened his practice, while also refashioning his public image. He moved ahead with writing, editing the journal *Haichaoyin*, setting up Buddhist seminaries, and planning new organizations. By the time he accidentally founded a worldwide Buddhist association and made his trip to Japan, many of these efforts were collapsing. His editorial work on *Haichaoyin* had exposed him to Tang Dayuan's proposal for a modernized form of *nianfo* practice that would lead to the "new Pure Land." Zang Guanchan's letters reinforced the need to think about instantiating the Pure Land in the present world.

Meanwhile, China had undergone the overthrow of the Qing dynasty, the repressive presidency of Yuan Shikai, and, when he fell from power, a relapse into local warlordism that roiled the countryside with constant fighting. Many intellectuals were thinking about ways to improve things while the people suffered greatly. However, the year 1926, when Taixu published his Essay, proved pivotal. Chiang Kai-shek embarked on the Northern Expedition that would rapidly bring all the warlords to heel and inaugurate a period of relative peace known as the "Nanjing Decade" (1927–37). During this time, Buddhist cultural activities would flourish in the cities of the Eastern Seaboard and China enjoyed a breathing spell before the Communist movement and Japan's invasion brought the country back to a state of war. When Taixu wrote his Essay in 1926, the Republican government had not yet begun the task of determining its religious policies (Nedostup 2009, 16), leaving Taixu free to imagine an ideal cooperative relationship between Buddhism and the state. This dream of Buddhism working closely with the government and receiving its full support pervades the vision of the Essay.

Thus, Taixu composed his Essay right at a turning point in his life and the country's fortunes. As we will see, its combination of anarchist utopian thinking and tales of Buddhist paradises, Buddhist communities built upon institutional planning and bodhisattva vows, and appeals to engage with the problems of the present world combined with hopes for ideal future rebirths brings all of these elements together. The constant turmoil and fighting of local warlords after the end of Yuan Shikai's rule brought about tremendous dislocation and suffering, and one can see Taixu's sense of compassion and urgency in the cries of "alas!" and calls to action found throughout the Essay. In its pages, he sought to offer hope for the people, both by engaging with the problems of the present and by holding out hope for rebirth in a distant blessed future. It is very much a document that reflects Taixu's life and thought and responds to China's political vicissitudes.

We will end our biographical survey here. Jiang Canteng has asserted that Taixu's life, which extended another twenty years beyond this point, had reached a new watershed (Jiang 1993, 215). However, our purpose here has simply been to contextualize the Essay by placing it within the arcs of Taixu's life and modern Chinese history. With that done, we may now move on to a survey of past Western writings on Taixu and an analysis of the Essay's contents.

3

Previous Western Writings on Taixu's Ideas about the "Pure Land in the Human Realm"

From the beginning, Western scholars viewed Taixu as a modernizer and secularizer because these were the only features of his activities and publications that early observers reported. For various reasons, his early involvement with anarchism and radical politics remained hidden from view (Ritzinger 2017, 28), and so that facet of his life did not figure in earlier accounts of his life and activities. In addition, since scholars thought traditional Buddhist beliefs and practices were incompatible with modernization, they either ignored Taixu's association with the former or claimed that he was not sincere about it. As noted above, the Norwegian missionary Karl L. Reichelt met Taixu in the mid-1920s and observed his activities for several years. He faithfully reported that Taixu's missionary chapel in Hankou had an image of Amitābha in it and that its gatherings included group buddha-recitation practice (*nianfo*); however, he ascribed this to Taixu's desire to duplicate the successful methods of the Christian missionaries and his judgment that the Chinese masses wanted it. "[Taixu], who actually had little use for the ways of faith and worship, found it expedient to use this method as a preparation with the crowds" (Reichelt 1954, 80–1). The last chapter of Reichelt's *The Transformed Abbot* gives a brief biography of Taixu that reports only his early revolutionary activities and his later efforts to modernize Buddhism while neglecting Taixu's more traditional proclivities (Reichelt 1954, 152–7).

Similarly, in *The Chinese Recorder* of 1923, the Presbyterian missionary Frank R. Millican tells his readers that in one conversation he pointed out to Taixu that Buddhism had no savior figure to help powerless human beings. In response, Taixu said there was indeed such a figure in Buddhism, but he "did not seem to be very strong on this point … Emphasis on faith in another as a means of salvation as we find it in the writings of … adherents of the Pure Land Sect is conspicuous by its absence from the writings of [Taixu]" (Millican 1923, 331).

Note here that Taixu actually answered Millican's query in the affirmative, and that Millican's evidence for his conclusion consists solely in his own opinion that Taixu lacked enthusiasm. Also, while Taixu may not have written much about Pure Land practice prior to 1923, he had not been completely silent about it; recall that his *Proposal*, written during his seclusion, included Pure Land as one of the eight schools of Chinese Buddhism and spoke approvingly of it. He brings it up very positively in later writings, such as the Essay under consideration here.

Clarence Hamilton, a philosophy professor in Nanjing, encountered Taixu unexpectedly at Mount Lu a few years later. During their impromptu conversation, Hamilton got the impression that Taixu had little use for images of buddhas and bodhisattvas, but kept them "because he believes it is necessary for the common people to have some image to which they can turn their thoughts" (Hamilton 1928, 165).

All three of these interlocutors agreed that Taixu's use of Pure Land images and practices was a sham display that he utilized only as an expedient for attracting "the masses" and "the common people." They observed and duly noted that Taixu used traditional Buddhist rituals, practices, and images, and even reported his own positive comments regarding them, as in his response to Millican. Nevertheless, they presented him primarily as an agent of modernization, and to explain these discordant facts they imputed to him a derogatory attitude toward these elements and toward people they considered uneducated and lower-class. The Essay will show that he harbored a sincere respect for all traditional Buddhist schools.

Paul Callahan, one of the earliest secular academic writers to report on Republican-era Buddhism, also portrayed Taixu exclusively as a modernizer in his 1952 report on the reformer's activities. Callahan's focus on Taixu's modernization program was so single-minded that he ignored even the counterevidence contained in his paper. For example, in delineating Taixu's reform program, Callahan noted that besides encouraging social engagement, restructuring the *sangha*, land reform, and so on, Taixu also advocated the use of buddha-images to encourage the masses, esoteric rituals, and *nianfo* ("muttering of prayers and names of the Buddha," quoted from Taixu 1925, 181). He also reproduces a report stating that Taixu preceded one of his public lectures with an "impressive act of worship" (Callahan 1952, 156). Even so, he concludes: "To one versed in traditional Buddhism, such a program seems rather un-Buddhistic, a far cry from the 'other-worldliness' usually associated with Buddhism" (Callahan 1952, 158–9). Put syllogistically, real Buddhism is otherworldly; Taixu's Buddhism is not otherworldly; therefore, Taixu's Buddhism is "un-Buddhistic."

Most Western scholars first became aware of Taixu's importance through the groundbreaking work of Holmes Welch, who devoted a chapter of *The Buddhist Revival in China* to Taixu (Welch 1968, 51–71). In this work, Welch portrays Taixu primarily as an organizer and modernizer, and not a very good one at that. While acknowledging (briefly and citing Reichelt) that Taixu's ministry utilized Pure Land elements, Welch contends that Taixu did not use them out of any genuine devotion on his part, but grudgingly included them as a sop for ignorant followers who knew nothing better (Welch 1968, 68). Welch's characterization dominated the Western scholarly understanding of Taixu's role in Buddhist modernism for a long time.

Don Pittman, in the first monograph-length study of Taixu, retained this interpretation. His summation of Taixu's "On the Establishment of the Pure Land in the Human Realm" omits all references to traditional Pure Land and Maitreyan themes and focuses primarily on the plan for an ideal Buddhist community. In his conclusions, Pittman lists Joseph Kitagawa's three hallmarks of modern religion, the second of which is an abandonment of otherworldly or postmortem paradises in favor of work in the present world, and he states that Taixu meets this description: "[Taixu] understood the significance of human existence, emphasized the attainment of buddhahood within this world, and rejected the givenness of the social order in favor of building a pure land on earth" (Pittman 2001, 294). As the translation of the Essay herein will demonstrate, this assertion mischaracterizes Taixu's thought.

A recent doctoral dissertation by Eric Goodell and a monograph by Justin Ritzinger have expanded our understanding of Taixu and shown him to be a character of greater complexity than that presented in earlier studies. Goodell makes note of the influence that Taixu's grandmother's practice of *nianfo* had on him (Goodell 2012, 20) and the importance of his early experiences in meditation. He grants that Taixu recognized Pure Land as a legitimate school of Chinese Buddhism (Goodell 2012, 82) and that after 1928 (by which time the Northern Expedition had reunited China and made nationwide organization possible again), Taixu softened his criticism of more traditionalist forms of practice in an effort to smooth his relationships with older influential monks (Goodell 2012, 207.). However, for Goodell, Taixu remains a modernizer whose tolerance of traditional practices was merely tactical:

> Taixu was not so much interested in reducing the influence of the incense-offering Buddhists, but rather in demonstrating to new Buddhists that their understanding of Buddhism was more genuine, and unrelated to the more

traditional type. In this connection, Taixu's *Humanistic Science* disparages the devotional masses who see buddhas and bodhisattvas as gods and seek heavenly rewards. (Goodell 2012, 198)

Ritzinger is much more expansive in the matter of Taixu's devotional life. The book shows that Taixu nurtured a lifelong devotion to Maitreya and sincerely sought to gain rebirth in the Tuṣita Heaven when he died. He promoted Maitreya worship when he could and provided Maitreyan devotional liturgies for his followers within the institutions that he founded (Ritzinger 2017, chs. 3, 4). We will see this in Taixu's declaration in his Essay that, even after years of social engagement, practitioners must still face their inevitable deaths and prepare for their future rebirths. Ritzinger's assessment of Taixu's feelings regarding Amitābha Pure Land practice is somewhat ambiguous, however. Was Taixu content to let Buddhists conduct practices leading to rebirth in Sukhāvatī rather than the Tuṣita Heaven, or did he simply resign himself to its inevitability given its overwhelming and longstanding popularity? Ritzinger does not provide his insights into these questions, but when we examine the themes of the Essay in Chapter 5, we will see that Taixu appears to give equal weight to both Amitābha and Maitreya practices.

We can see the effect of this scholarship when we look at the work of other academics who, while not specializing in the study of Taixu themselves, cite the above works for their own research in modern Chinese Buddhism. By and large, they have adopted the prevailing view of Taixu as a modernizer who deplored traditional Buddhist practice, as these three examples will show. Richard Madsen, in his book *Democracy's Dharma*, says "Monks like Tai Xu (*sic*) strove to interpret Mahayana Buddhism in this-worldly terms. Instead of hoping to go to some heavenly pure land after death, Buddhists should place their hope on making this world a pure land by devoting themselves to eliminating social suffering" (Madsen 2007, 23).

David Schak's synopsis of Taixu's thought is similar:

Socially engaged Buddhism grew out of the teachings of a very influential monastic, Ven. Taixu (1890–1947). Ven. Taixu was very dissatisfied with the state of Buddhism. He wanted to move it away from its dependency on funerals, rituals to appease spirits and repeating Amithaba's (*sic*) name to earn merit for others and ensure their rebirth in the pure land. He also hoped to make this world into the pure land by working in and improving society. Buddhism, he argued, needed to concentrate on accumulating merit in this life. (Xu et al. 2007, 202–3)

Finally, in explaining the historical sources of modern Chinese Buddhism, Raoul Birnbaum describes Taixu in this way:

> In contrast to this [fundamentalist] response, the seemingly tireless monk Taixu (1889–1947) proposed a programme of comprehensive modernizing. ... Taixu was strongly driven by his understanding of modernity, which in part was conceived as Westernization. He hoped to induce a radical modernization of the Buddhist sangha, in which the numbers would be greatly reduced and the level of learning greatly increased. Taixu was concerned with creating a 20th-century Buddhism—which included notions of religion derived from Christian models, as well as notions of Buddhism derived from European academic assumptions. ... He also was strongly encouraged by relations with foreigners, especially Protestant missionaries in China, who cheered on his rhetoric of "anti-superstition," drastic clerical reform and social action. ... In contrast to the step back from worldly engagement of the [conservative] practitioners, Taixu sought to reconstruct the Buddhist clergy as an elite corps of men and women who would deeply engage with the world as it was encountered, and seek to change it. Taixu wanted to get rid of the buddhas and bodhisattvas, and eliminate the funerary rites that were a principal source of income for some clerics and their monasteries. The buddhas and bodhisattvas in their guise as celestial benefactors are illusions, as is the Western Paradise of Amita [i.e., Amitābha] Buddha, to which so many Chinese Buddhist devotees seek rebirth. He proposed that superstition-free Buddhists turn this place right here into a pure land, by bright mental training and compassionate activity. (Birnbaum 2003, 434–6)

We could cite other examples (e.g., Tymick 2014 and Pacey 2014), but this will do for now.

I should note that it is not just Western scholars who present Taixu exclusively in this light; Chinese scholars are also prone to this bias. For example, in an article tracing the concept of "Humanistic Buddhism" from Taixu to Yinshun and Xingyun, the Taiwan scholar Cai Zhennian 蔡振念 summarized Taixu's thoughts in "On the Establishment of the Pure Land in the Human Realm" as a simple matter of having people practice Buddhist virtues within society and purify their minds, after which a pure land would manifest here and now. In reference to Taixu's Essay, Cai points specifically to material found in the 1930 appendix, saying that Taixu only advocated (1) using governmental offices to establish education, the arts, and morals on a legal basis and (2) binding the country together within Buddhism (Cai 2017, 81).

However, these distortions have not intruded into all studies by East Asian scholars. For instance, Jiang Canteng 江燦騰 published a critical biography of Taixu's early life in which he notes that the monk constantly "fluctuated" (*paihuai* 徘徊) between the modern and the traditional (Jiang 1993, 212). Hong Jinlian 洪金蓮 expressed the same thought, though more charitably, when she wrote that Taixu was both one of the most accomplished traditional Buddhists of his day, but also the one who instigated Buddhism's modernization (Hong 1999, 339).

What seems common to Western analyses is the tendency to split the Republican period Buddhist world into two opposing camps: traditionalist monks and the "Buddhist masses" or "common people" on one side, and the reformers and modernizers on the other. Left out is a middle group of monks and laymen who were educated and prosperous members of modern urban society, but nevertheless wanted to participate in more traditional practices such as Pure Land. Brooks Jessup's 2010 dissertation shows that even as they agreed with reformers that the Buddhist clergy needed reconstruction and went about setting up their own lay Buddhist societies in Shanghai, such organizations included sutra-chanting and *nianfo* as daily practices (Jessup 2010, ch. 1). Thus, I would contend that Taixu never intended to make the elimination of such practices part of his modernization program, nor did he need to deploy them disingenuously simply to gain the support of "the masses." Urban Buddhist laypeople wanted them, and, as seen in Taixu's Essay and in the Christian missionary reports of his activities, he was happy to provide rationales for them. Seen in this light, his copious use of sutra citations and his endorsement of Pure Land practices and cosmology in the Essay make perfect sense, and the reader, no longer constrained by the image of Taixu as the avatar of modernization, has no further need to explain them away.

4

Utopianism East and West in Taixu's Essay

As indicated in the first chapter, I initially approached Taixu's Essay prepared by previous scholarship to see modernization and reform as its major thrust. Ritzinger's analysis of Taixu also prepared me to encounter Taixu's hybrid anarchist-Buddhist vision for the "Great Unity." Nevertheless, the Essay contained many elements that confounded these expectations, one of which came in a section entitled "The Establishment of a Pure Land in the Human Realm" (*Renjian jingtu zhi jianshe* 人間淨土之建設), in which Taixu presented several examples of past utopian literature. Among the six categories of text that he catalogued, I found the following two especially intriguing:

5. The ideal states of Socrates and Plato, the *Utopia* of Thomas More,[1] the *Nova Atlantis* of Francis Bacon, Tommaso Campanella's The *City of the Sun*, and James Harrington's *The Commonwealth of Oceana* are all examples of ancient Western thinkers' desiderata for constructing a Pure Land in the Human Realm.
6. [Edward] Bellamy's [novel] *Looking Backward*, [Theodor] Hertzka's *Freeland* [: *A Social Anticipation*], and [H. G.] Wells' [novel] *A Modern Utopia* all exemplify modern thinkers and their desiderata for establishing a Pure Land in the Human Realm.

How did Taixu know about these works? Were they circulating in Chinese translation? Had he read them himself? I began looking for clues connecting Taixu and these Western utopian works and thinking about the ways in which they might have influenced his thinking.

---

[1] Thomas More (1478–1535) completed the *Utopia* in 1516 while in prison. In it, a visitor describes to More a place called Utopia in which there is no private property, everyone holds all things in common, and dines together in a great hall. See Baker-Smith (2014).

Utopias and Paradises: A Crucial Distinction

This investigation began with a look at past scholarship on Western utopian writing. In this literature, I found that researchers generally drew a technical distinction between a "utopia" and other sorts of idealized environments that I will group under the name "paradises." A "utopia" would be a society that human beings designed and implemented for themselves. In a typical work of utopian fiction, a traveler from the author's society stumbles into a small-scale community that appears to be remarkably well-run and peaceful. A local denizen explains to the traveler how the community was set up, the social contract that governs its activities and relations, the means employed for regulating behavior, agricultural and industrial practices, and various other features. These schemes are always entirely secular; utopias come into being solely by dint of human effort and ingenuity unaided by divine direction or intervention. Aside from presenting a presumably better alternative to prevailing social structures and relations, this literature often serves to satirize the author's own society (Kumar 1987, 104–9).

A "paradise," on the other hand, simply exists, either because it has already been established by divine forces (e.g., the Garden of Eden, the Christian Heaven, or the Pure Land of Amitābha), or because it just happened to evolve as an ideal place that required no social engineering to design its idyllic life (such as Uttarakuru). No human being had a hand in its design or actualization. Since all human desires are provided for spontaneously, there is no competition or crime and thus no need for a constitution to organize distribution or laws to regulate behavior.

This distinction matters because Taixu's Essay, while at first glance a piece of utopian writing, actually describes *both* utopias *and* paradises. He even makes this distinction himself when he writes thus:

> [The need to secure life and property] gives rise to two types [of response]: First, [people] search for a pure realm outside the present world, such as rebirth in a heavenly land as taught in the theistic religions or in a Pure Land elsewhere as taught in Buddhism. Second, imagining how the present world could be made more ideal through local government, they hope to establish it by implementing reforms. (Taixu 1956, 24:395)

When he proposes plans for an idealized Buddhist mountaintop community and when in the last section he sets forth desiderata for reforming the present world, he is engaged in utopian speculation. But he also talks about life in the mythical northern continent of Uttarakuru, the Inner Court of Maitreya in the Tuṣita Heaven, and the western buddha-land Sukhāvatī. More interestingly, in his description of Uttarakuru he shuttles back and forth between depicting Uttarakuru as a paradise and as a model utopia that humanity might one day simulate through technology.

Although I will venture some detailed conjectures about why Taixu mixes utopian planning and paradisiacal description in a single text in this chapter's conclusion, it seems expedient to foreshadow the argument here. As many scholars of utopian literature have noted, utopias are always secular, while paradises are either religious or neutral. Zhang Longxi states that because of this, some researchers in the past have asserted that it is a genre that could only arise in the climate of the European Renaissance and Enlightenment and needed the rejection of the idea of paradise as a precondition; other civilizations did not divorce religion from politics enough to produce it (Zhang 2002, 3–6). I will not enter the debate on whether or not China had any utopian thinkers or literature before the nineteenth century. Here I will simply note my agreement with the proposition that utopian literature is inherently secular in nature, and thus could not accommodate Taixu's religious impulses. At the same time, his own experience with anarchism and his desire to refit Buddhism to meet modern needs dictated that he could not base all his plans on the purely religious hope for a paradise to be gained here or elsewhere. To be true to his vision, the Pure Land in the Human Realm *had* to amalgamate, however uneasily, both utopian and paradisiacal features.

The Inherent Ambiguity of Utopias

Scholars who analyze this literature have also pointed to another feature of utopian writing that began to appear about the time that Taixu composed his Essay. Such writing became highly ambiguous; one may wonder whether the society being described is truly a utopia or a dystopia (Kumar 1987, ch. 4). One reason for this ambiguity derives from a common trope of utopian fiction: the inhabitants of the ideal society exhibit an unusual uniformity of thought and are "of one heart and mind" in all things. While this sounds splendid, early twentieth-century writers wondered how they achieved such a state of harmony (see Levitas 1990, 185). Indeed, as Douwe Fokkema points out, the status of a work as utopian or dystopian may vary from reader to reader, depending upon the value system each brings to their reading (Fokkema 2011, 345, 398).

In a representative novel, Evgeny Zamyatin's *We*, uniformity is achieved through a medical procedure that renders citizens incapable of being unhappy with their social and political situation. The coercion needed to gain this harmonious state might even entail mass killing and genocide ("Everything will be perfect once we get these people out of the way."). I will return to this point in the conclusions and speculate on how Taixu seemed to be aware of this problem and took steps to neutralize it.

First, let us ask how Taixu became cognizant of Western utopian fiction.

Utopianism in Republican China

I found my first clue in Wolfgang Bauer's book *China and the Search for Happiness*. Bauer pointed out that some earlier Chinese groups, such as the Taiping rebels, had already put forth plans for a utopian social order that showed some awareness of Western ideas (Bauer 1976, 293). More significantly, Bauer highlighted a book that appeared in China in 1926, the same year that Taixu published his Essay on the Pure Land in the Human Realm. A work introduced in Chapter 2, Liu Renhang's 劉仁航 two-volume work called *Case Studies of Datong in the East* (*Dongfang datong xue'an* 東方大同學案) based its assessment of Western utopian works on Joyce Hertzler's 1923 *History of Utopian Thought* (Bauer 1976, 331–2). An examination of Hertzler's book shows that she wrote about the same works that appear in Taixu's list given above (Hertzler 1923, ch. 4: "The Early Modern Utopians"). Liu, being very proficient in English, would have been able to read Hertzler's book with relative ease.

When I obtained a copy of Liu's book, I discovered two things. First, Hertzler's study did indeed appear in its bibliography. Second, Taixu himself had provided a preface for it. From this preface I found that Taixu had known Liu Renhang since his years of seclusion at Mount Putuo (1914–17), when Liu had sent him copies of *Bao'en xueshe congzhu* 報恩學社叢著 (Works of the Merit-Requiting Society) and *Guanyin futianyuan yuanqi shige* 觀音福田院緣起詩歌 (Poems on the Wonders of the Guanyin Futian Hall). As we saw in Taixu's biography, Liu was also one of the charter members of the Bodhi Society in Shanghai. A decade later, when Taixu went to Japan to attend the Great Eastern Buddhist Conference, Liu Renhang dispatched a family member to give Taixu a copy of his manuscript for his appraisal. Taixu reports only perusing the table of contents, but says that it convinced him that Liu had read widely enough about the cultures of India, China, and Europe to make an adequate comparison of all their utopian aspirations. The strength of the book, he says, is that while it brings forward the advantages of each of these three religious cultures and shows how they complement each other, it also affirms that Buddhism represents the *telos* and fulfillment of all of them (Liu 1926, 1:1–2[2]).

This raises an interesting question: Did Taixu actually read Liu's book? By his own account he only looked through the table of contents while participating in an international conference that kept him quite busy. In addition, upon reading *Case Studies*, one finds that, despite the inclusion of Hertzler's book in its bibliography, it treats different utopian texts than those found in Taixu's Essay, and even when discussing works that appear in both his and Taixu's works, the two men render the English titles of the works into different Chinese characters. One tantalizing clue indicates that Taixu may have read more than just the contents, however. In his Essay, Taixu inserts a quotation attributed to Laozi under the name Lao Dan (老聃), but the quotation actually comes from another ancient Daoist text, the *Liezi* 列子 (Taixu 1956, 24:392–3). The passage appears in Liu's book (1b:99), where the reference to Lao Dan is part of the citation itself and not, as in Taixu's quotation, a mistaken attribution. In other words, the *Liezi* quotes from Lao Dan, but Taixu places the attribution to the latter before the quotation as part of its introduction. Thus, it remains unclear to what extent Liu Renhang's *Case Studies* provided the source material for Taixu's citations of Western utopian literature. Given their long association, it may be that Liu influenced Taixu more through conversations and letters than through *Case Studies*.

It is likely that Liu Renhang was not Taixu's only source. Wolfgang Bauer reports that in the early years of the twentieth century, translations of several Western utopian novels entered the Chinese market (Bauer 1976, 331–2), and in an instance within the Essay Taixu does show familiarity with one of the Western utopian novels he had listed earlier. His quotation from the *Sutra on the Arising of Worlds* describes the forests of Uttarakuru as having foliage so dense that rain does not reach the ground, keeping all the inhabitants dry and comfortable. In his insertion following this, Taixu says: "Note: The book *Looking Backward, 2000-1887* [by Edward Bellamy] advocates that there be a common covering over cities that would keep out the rain but let

---

[2] Following Liu's convention, Taixu indicates these religious cultures by using the swastika for India, the *yin-yang* symbol for China, and the cross for the West. Also, Liu's book appears in two volumes, but each volume is divided into books, and it begins the pagination from 1 in each. Thus, citations from *Case Studies* will indicate volume, book, and page.

the breezes through. These trees are very similar in function" (Taixu 1956, 24:358). This is the only indication in the Essay that Taixu had read one of these Western works.

Even without direct knowledge of these novels, however, Taixu's vision was influenced by the effect that their translation and circulation had on Chinese intellectual culture. Douwe Fokkema tells us that their appearance, playing off the social turmoil of the early Republican period, altered the form of Chinese utopian literature along more Western lines, notably by injecting the theme of technological futurism into them (Fokkema 2011, 277). Prior to that time, Chinese stories of idyllic societies tended to look backward, depicting pastoral societies unspoiled by the encroachments of modern technology and social problems. Now Chinese writers began looking forward to future utopias that human engineering, both social and technological, would bring into being.

Against this background, and knowing that his involvement in anarchism predisposed Taixu toward (or reinforced his predilection toward) utopian planning, what do we find in the Essay?

Utopian Visions in Taixu's Essay

Within the Essay, one finds Taixu describing both utopias and paradises of various sorts. Very early on, he quotes the entire section of the *Sutra on the Arising of Worlds* (*Qishi yinben jing* 起世因本經, T.24) describing the paradisiacal northern continent of Uttarakuru (Taixu 1956, 24:357–2). While it exhibits many of the common tropes of Western utopianism—free love, communal child-rearing, a moneyless system of distribution, abundance of all life's requisites—it is a paradise and not a utopia. The people who inhabit it had no hand in designing or constructing its wonders; it is simply a world into which their past good karma has led them.

However, Taixu sprinkles the citation with his own comments, which show that all the marvelous features of Uttarakuru could conceivably be replicated in the future by human artifice. For example, a passage that appears early in the quotation indicates that the trees of Uttarakuru spontaneously produce dishes, food, and flame-emitting jewels that cook the food to perfection. Taixu inserts two notes into this passage. First, with regard to the flaming jewels, he says, "Note: these are clearly modern electric, coal, or gas stoves." Shortly thereafter, he comments on this entire system of food-provision as follows:

> Note: This clearly says "dish-producing trees" and "ruby flames" so that one knows it [appears] by the Buddha's supernatural powers, [but] one can also plainly see today's mechanized world. In their massive form one can see today's mechanized factories, and the branches are just the conduits. People generally take [talk of] worlds like this where material culture is perfect as empty prattle. How wrong they are! (Taixu 1956, 24:360)

Another amusing example appears later, when the sutra says that when anyone needs to urinate or defecate in that land, the ground opens up to reveal running water that carries the waste away and then closes back up. To this Taixu inserts the remark "This would be a flush toilet" (Taixu 1956, 24:371). In this way, Taixu treats Uttarakuru both as a paradise and a utopia, a place into which one may land by dint of good karma and a template for an ideal country that human beings have already begun to design and build.

Taixu strikes a discordant note (to modern sensibilities) when he makes clear that his vision of a technology capable of creating a paradise-like world includes eugenics (*youshengxue* 優生學). The following section of the sutra's description of Uttarakuru and Taixu's comment upon it may give the reader pause:

> O monks! The people of Uttarakuru all have sky-blue hair eight fingers in length. All the people are of the same kind, the same form, the same color. There are no other forms or colors by which to differentiate them. — [Taixu's note:] This is extremely important. The races of humans evolved, and the inferior races were eliminated (*taotai liezhong* 淘汰劣種). These days everyone is discussing eugenics just for this purpose. — (Taixu 1956, 24:367)

It thus appears that the vision of the Great Unity (*Datong* 大同) has no room for diversity, a point one may easily miss if one skips over the sutra quotations when reading the Essay.

The section of the Essay detailing his plan for an ideal Buddhist community follows the outlines of a Western utopian vision most closely (Taixu 1956, 24:399–403). As with most utopias, it has a limited population (he envisioned about 20,000 inhabitants) in a secluded area cut off from the world at large, in this case a mountain with a clear boundary and a gatehouse. Within this community, there would be a cadre of monks and nuns living in a set of temples at the top, while the lay population would be assigned to villages according to the level of Buddhist precepts they had undertaken. There would be a Three Refuges village, a Five Lay Precepts village, and a Ten Virtues village. As the level of commitment and precepts inhabitants undertake increases, tracts of land would be allocated closer to the center and be bigger. Taixu gives several details about the economic life of this community, its political arrangements, its traffic with the outside world, and the means by which it would elect its leadership and police its premises. In all its details, it is a true utopia, the product of unaided human planning.

However, the theme of paradise quickly returns to center stage. Immediately following the description of his Buddhist community, Taixu says this:

> The Pure Land in the Human Realm safeguards life and property by means of the Three Refuges and the Ten Virtues, and puts the Three Refuges and Ten Virtues into practice by safeguarding life and property, but that is all. One may extend one's life, but life still comes to an end and one dies. Since we believe that consciousness continues, takes on another body, and does not rest in oblivion, we thus must arrange for the "consciousness that continues to be embodied" a stable and appropriate basis in order to avoid the danger of going from delusion to delusion while bobbing up and down in samsara. However, having laid down the good roots of the Pure Land in the Human Realm based on the Three Refuges and the Ten Virtues, with the additional practice of invocation and transfer of merit, we gain ascent and rebirth in a pure land, either that of the Inner Court [of Maitreya] or of the [Land of] Utmost Bliss [of Amitābha] in the next life. One can examine the holy teachings for their testimony [of this]. (Taixu 1956, 24:404–5)

The two long sections that follow consist of long scripture citations that describe these two Buddhist realms and give advice on the means of attaining rebirth within them. These are paradises not created by human planning and skill.

Thus, we see that Taixu's vision of the ideal human community, the Pure Land in the Human Realm, both does and does not adhere to the canons of utopian writing. The "human realm" is any place within the Buddhist cosmos in which humans dwell: this Earth, Uttarakuru, the Pure Land of Amitābha, and the Inner Court of Maitreya. The ideal society may be a paradise gained by the accumulation of good karma and the setting forth of vows, or it might be a utopia brought forth by social planning and technological innovation on the part of human beings. How are we to understand this blurring of categories?

Understanding the Pure Land in the Human Realm

To answer this question, I wish to return to three features of utopian schemes noted earlier: their secular nature, the problem of uniting human hearts and minds without instituting a repressive regime, and the place of technology. I will also bring in another problem inherent in utopian communities: boredom and lack of purpose. I believe that Taixu mixed utopian and paradisiacal elements in order to address the problems entailed by utopianism alone and to keep Buddhism relevant to his vision.

Taixu's Essay may prove that utopias are indeed secular by the simple fact that he inserted paradises into his plan. Had he limited his thought to the strictly utopian, then the portion of the Essay devoted to envisioning an ideal society would have been restricted to the charter for his mountaintop community and the dream that technology might someday make possible the life of Uttarakuru. Like all utopias, these would be brought about solely by the exercise of human effort, invention, and social engineering, leaving no room for any Buddhist element to them at all. A strictly human design might prove highly flawed, as Taixu points out in his Essay:

> If the foundational principles are false, then the method will be riddled with errors and the search for ideal government based on them often devolves more and more into a destructive human environment. If on Marxism and materialism, it devolves into "going red" (*chihua* 赤化) characterized by class struggle as in the previous examples. (Taixu 1956, 24:395)

However, when he turns to the paradises—Uttarakuru, the Inner Court of the Tuṣita Heaven, the Pure land of Amitābha—he forces the introduction of religious conceptions, values, and practices. One attains rebirth in Uttarakuru by the meritorious karma of the Ten Virtuous Deeds. One joins Maitreya in his Inner Court by meditation and the creation of karmic linkages. One goes to the Pure Land of Amitābha when he comes to the deathbed to escort one there in response to one's practice of *nianfo*. The introduction of paradises alongside utopias makes religious practice relevant. Taixu justifies this move quite well when he points out that all the utopian world-building one may engage in while alive does not stave off death, and one must prepare for one's postmortem fate.

Taixu's emphasis on the Buddhist nature of his vision also helps to resolve the second problem common to utopian fantasies: the specter of totalitarianism. As mentioned above, utopian literature—both Western and Eastern—generally includes the stipulation that all the inhabitants of the ideal world are united in hearts and minds. They seem remarkably free from disagreement, dissension, and ideological diversity. How does any society achieve this without some form of coercion, without "thought police," and without the extermination of inconvenient populations of dissidents? In a religious paradise, the problem never arises. The inhabitants of Uttarakuru as described in the *Sutra on the*

Arising of Worlds seem uncannily free of any ideology at all; they spend their time in purely hedonistic pursuits. Those who attain rebirth in the Tuṣita Heaven or Sukhāvatī do so by a commitment to the life and goals of these places that they bring with them from their previous lives.

However, the mountain community that Taixu proposes in his Essay is a utopia, not a paradise, and in this connection, it matters that it is a *Buddhist* utopia. It will be cordoned off from the secular world, and those who wish to move in must submit to Buddhist beliefs and discipline. No one comes in who has not at least taken the Three Refuges, and once in, they move closer to the center and get larger allocations of land by taking more detailed and rigorous Buddhist vows. Celibate monks and nuns occupy the center. Thus, by stipulating a religious charter for this utopia, Taixu apparently hoped to achieve the spiritual unity typical of all utopian visions while averting any possible slide into a regime of thought control or coercion.

In the matter of technology as a means of bringing about utopia, the Western tradition was of two minds, and Taixu here appears to take a clear side. The Industrial Revolution and the sorry plight of factory workers led many to revile technology and dream of utopian societies freed from its curse. Karl Marx had said that industry had made the proletarian worker a mere "appendage to the machines," and Samuel Butler's utopian satire *Erewhon* depicted a society that had outlawed all machines (Kumar 1987, 106–9). On the other side, science-fiction writers beginning in the 1920s presented technology as part of the solution to humanity's problems. Technology and machines would ultimately free human beings from the monotony of factory work and yield the abundance of goods that would make life bearable if not beautiful. This optimism was on full display in the many World Fairs held during this period (Kumar 1987, 385–6). Taixu clearly belonged to this latter camp. Throughout the Essay, one sees an unwavering belief that technological development was the way forward, as long as it was tempered by religion, art, and education.

In sum, we may speculate that Ritzinger is correct in saying that Taixu brought the anarchist propensity for utopian thinking into his life as a Buddhist monk. We may also agree with Ritzinger that, as a Buddhist, Taixu blended it with the bodhisattva ideal of individual self-transformation. However, perhaps now we can say *why* he needed to blend these two programs in this particular way. He may have seen that an anarchist utopia ruled only by human effort and planning could easily become oppressive or suffer from a lack of purpose. The Buddhist plan for self-transformation, especially with its Mahayana emphasis on compassion, could create the spiritual unity that ideal societies need without resorting to coercion. By incorporating a religious vision undertaken voluntarily, the Pure Land in the Human Realm might indeed bring about a harmonious and happy social structure in which all live for all, while at the same time preserving human dignity and autonomy.

In addition, in the Essay Taixu is quite explicit about the problems raised by setting one's hope exclusively on either a paradise or a utopia. Theistic religions, he says, aim their adherents toward an eventual paradise such as the Christian Heaven. This is escapist, and leads people to turn their backs on the world. Utopian schemes, which he identifies with the Russian experiment with Communism, leads to authoritarianism and suffering because its lack of a religious vision gives free rein to the worst of human instincts (Taixu 1956, 24:395). As he looked about at the visions for reconstructing human society on offer in his day, he determined that only Buddhism had the right blend of social-structural reform and inner personal transformation needed to create an ideal world.

On a lighter note, we may add one more issue that utopias and paradises create besides the three already addressed: they tend to be pointless and boring. As the reader will see when reading the bucolic description of Uttarakuru in the Essay, its inhabitants move placidly through a very limited and purposeless set of pleasures each day: eating, bathing, procreating, resting. As Taixu says, even their 1,000-year lifespan ticks inexorably away, and in the end they have accomplished nothing. A utopia constructed according to a set of secular ideals also fades into a dull routine once all its structures and procedures are in place. That is why Taixu ultimately recommends living in a religiously founded utopia while alive and aiming for a Buddhist rebirth with Amitābha or Maitreya after death. In that way, one will continue working toward a meaningful goal both now and in the afterlife: buddhahood and the ceaseless exercise of compassionate action on behalf of all suffering beings.

Conclusion

Krishan Kumar tells us that, like Taixu, Fyodor Dostoyevsky had been an anarchist during his youth in the 1840s. Like Taixu, this had led him to invest much energy into utopian planning. After his arrest and exile, he lost all confidence that human beings could plan and implement a perfect society without the threat of lapsing into authoritarianism and tyranny. Then he had a religious conversion, after which he began once again to think about a way to build a utopia in a Christian key (Kumar 1987, 124).

This shows us that Taixu's trajectory is not unique. It may well be that all purely secular utopian schemes entail the risks of coercion in their construction and boredom in their realization. If this is the case, then the injection of religious elements into such schemes, their re-sacralization if you will, renews the hope that human society can attain perfection. Religion will build the consensus that otherwise would require suppression and massacre to achieve, and a common religious quest might address the problems of meaninglessness and boredom. If Taixu had had a chance to build his mountain community, then the inhabitants' commitment to Buddhist ideals might have given them the union of hearts and minds necessary for harmonious relations, and the continual self-transformation mandated by the bodhisattva ideal would provide interest and purpose. His vision went beyond setting up a single human community here on earth. In his mind, his mountaintop utopia would bring together people who already shared a vision, would give them purpose as they advanced inward in self-transformation and outward in missionary work, and lead them together to a Buddhist paradise after death where they could continue their progress.

5

Key Themes

Before turning to the translation, we will review some of the primary concerns that animate Taixu's Essay and provide the reader with contextualization to assist in understanding its contents.

Where Is the "Human Realm"?

The English phrase "Human Realm" has always struck me as a clumsy rendering of the Chinese term *renjian* 人間, but no other translation serves as well to prevent misunderstanding. If one has been predisposed by earlier studies to read Taixu only as a reformer or modernizer who wanted his followers to work for the betterment of society here and now, then translations of *renjian jingtu* 人間淨土 such as "human Pure Land" or "Earthly Pure Land" might seem adequate. If Taixu's main concern is reform and upliftment in the present world, then why would one translate it another way? However, if one keeps in mind that Taixu retained many aspects of traditional Buddhist cosmology as noted above, then the inappropriateness of such translations stands out clearly.

In the premodern Buddhist universe, human beings form one of the five or six paths of rebirth along with hell-beings, hungry ghosts, animals, (sometimes) *asuras* (semidivine beings lower than *devas*), and *devas*. Within this cosmology, the planet Earth is not the only place one may find humans. The Pure Land sutras state that *devas* and humans occupy Amitābha's Land of Bliss as well as the pure lands of other buddhas. The northern continent of Uttarakuru also has human inhabitants living in ideal conditions. Taixu's Essay reflects this traditional conception of the human rebirth, and so any translation of *renjian* that implies that this form of rebirth occurs only on the planet Earth leads us astray. Accordingly, I determined that something akin to "the Human Realm," awkward as it might sound, translates the term as Taixu employs it most accurately.

Thus, when reading through the Essay, the reader should not be surprised to find Taixu talking about the Pure Land in the Human Realm as more than just a possible outcome of social improvement and technological advances here on Earth. In various parts of the Essay, he states explicitly that Uttarakuru, the Pure Land, other buddha-fields, and the abode of Maitreya all encompass populations of human beings. He also discusses it as a state of rebirth to be found on Earth but in a distant future when Maitreya descends and achieves buddhahood billions of years from now. If one approaches the Essay as a call to Buddhists of the present age to abandon otherworldly goals in order to carry out reforms here and now, one will miss the fullness of Taixu's vision. The "Human Realm" is much more expansive in space and time than that.

Human Needs and Their Fulfillment in Pure Land

From the very opening of the Essay, Taixu announces that human beings have very real and immediate needs for security of life and property, along with future needs for immortality and bliss. These arise from the two forms in which past karma ripens and manifests. The first is "proper recompense" (*zheng bao* 正報), which includes all aspects of past karma that affect one personally by manifesting in traits such as height, gender, intelligence, and all other individual characteristics. For this, one seeks security and long life in the present, and immortality after death. The second is "dependent recompense" (*yi bao* 依報), which manifests as environmental factors that affect one's quality of life. This includes the place into which one is reborn, one's family, one's wealth, availability of Buddhist teachers, and so on. In the process of looking for optimal conditions for one's life, one seeks security of property now, and later one tries to attain a blissful state in which all requisites of life come into one's possession with minimal effort and without fear of deprivation.

The drive to gain the advantages of security and property without the restraints and wisdom of religion leads to evil results in the present world. As Taixu says,

> In order to extend their lives and pass it on to children and grandchildren, they protect their property by establishing households and countries. Unending complication arises from this. They go on to limitless future rebirths and all kinds of war and strife arise. Their very efforts to secure their lives and property become the very means by which life and property are lost. (Taixu 1956, 24:356)

Competition leads to wars which only further the loss of life and property, producing the very opposite of what people want. Taixu says this is "topsy-turvy" (*diandao* 顛倒) and points to Buddhist teachings that can lead seekers more directly to the fulfillment of these needs.

People may fulfill the first set of needs, those for security of life and property, by seeking rebirth in Uttarakuru, a place within Buddhist cosmology where human beings dwell in a hedonistic paradise and enjoy fixed lifespans of 1,000 years. While Taixu tries to accommodate this cosmology to modern science by stating that this is a planet in our solar system, he still presumes its literal existence and, following the sutra citation, says that one may attain rebirth there by practicing the Ten Virtues. However, he goes on to say that even a life span of 1,000 years comes to an end, and so Uttarakuru cannot meet the human need for immortality and bliss. Only rebirth in a pure buddha-land can bring that about.

He returns to this subject in section 2, noting there that human beings experience difficulty and suffering of three types: natural disasters, personal problems, and social problems. Rebirth in Uttarakuru can take care of the natural and social problems, but some personal problems will remain. In our present world, science and technology have made improvements in some areas of life, but people are still helpless when it comes to natural disasters and international competition. Once again, only rebirth in a pure buddha-land resolves all three issues and satisfies our need for a thoroughly blissful existence. Thus, even as Buddhists practice the Ten Virtues and strive to act compassionately to effect change in the world, they should understand that only rebirth in a buddha-realm resolves all possible human problems. This leads us to the next theme (Taixu 1956, 24:382–4).

The Compatibility of This-Worldly Work and Otherworldly Goals

As we saw when surveying previous scholarship on Taixu, most researchers believe that he sought to dissuade his readers from traditional Buddhist practices that aimed at rebirth in a Pure Land, considering such efforts pessimistic and escapist. In this reading, he used the term "Pure Land in the Human Realm" as a slogan by which to call his followers to work hard to create the Pure Land in our present world. While it is true that he expresses disapproval of an overly pessimistic view that considers our present world unsalvageable and seeks *only* to achieve the Pure Land after death, he saw no contradiction between the two efforts. One could do good in society all one's life and still aspire to a Buddhist-defined postmortem goal.

We presented a long quotation from the Essay to this effect in the previous chapter, so it is not necessary to cite it again. However, we should note its placement. Taixu's statement that human beings all die and need to devote some practice to attaining rebirth in the company of either Amitābha or Maitreya follows immediately after the lengthy description of his proposed Buddhist intentional community. By proceeding directly from laying out ideas for a Pure Land in this present Human Realm to long scripture citations that tell the reader how to achieve rebirth in one of these traditional domains after death, Taixu signals his conviction that these activities are not inherently at odds. On the contrary, the first leads smoothly into the second.

On a more philosophical level, Taixu argues that this-worldly activity comports with an aspiration for rebirth in a buddha-land without contradiction because, from the ultimate perspective, the two are nondual. In a later section in which he describes the "Pure Land of the Ocean of Awakening," he teaches that, from a buddha's enlightened point of view, all distinctions dissolve, thus removing even the conditions that make contradiction possible.

> In reliance upon the pure vows of Maitreya and Amitābha as contributory conditions, one quells the afflicted actions and increases pure actions leading to the purification of the mind of awakening, which then manifests as the pure lands of the Inner Court [of Maitreya in the Tuṣita Heaven] or the Pure Land of Utmost Bliss [of Amitābha]. Within the great ocean of the mind of awakening there is a small part not yet purified, thus one cannot thoroughly differentiate all characteristics. ... However, in order that bodhisattvas at all stages of progress may enjoy it together, along with those of the Three Vehicles and the Five Destinies, he also manifests all Pure and Impure bodies and lands as if by magical transformation with inexhaustible distinctions. Know that in the ocean of awakening, they are all together in the Pure Land! If one wishes to plumb the meaning of this, it is all contained in the teaching, principle, practices, and fruition of the Mahayana dharma. (Taixu 1956, 24:416)

Thus, this very land in which Mahayana Buddhists strive to bring benefit and relieve suffering as well as the Pure Lands to which their striving will lead them are equally manifested by the buddhas. When both the present field of struggle and the future pure buddha-lands interpenetrate within the Ocean of Awakening, what room is there for contradiction?

The Relationship between the Cults of Amitābha and Maitreya

As Justin Ritzinger has convincingly demonstrated, Taixu felt a particular affinity with the bodhisattva and future buddha Maitreya and engaged in practices aimed at going to the Inner Court of the Tuṣita Heaven to be in Maitreya's presence and form the karmic links necessary to accompany him when, in a far distant future, he descends to the Earth to attain buddhahood (Ritzinger 2017). This in itself belies the notion that Taixu rejected all premodern, "superstitious" beliefs and practices. Nevertheless, as seen above, Western scholars held that he rejected traditional Pure Land practices aimed at rebirth in Sukhāvatī with the Buddha Amitābha. Thus, even if we acknowledge that he did not reject any Buddhist practice as incompatible with modernity, we can still ask whether he promoted Maitreya devotionalism to the detriment of the more popular Pure Land cult.

Evidence from the Essay suggests that he held both paths to be equally valid. For example, section 4, called "The Pure Land in the Human Realm and Eternal Life and Utmost Bliss," is devoted entirely to describing the attractions of and conditions for rebirth in the pure lands of both Maitreya and Amitābha. After these quotations, he expresses no preference or claim of superiority for either. The reason, as he makes plain in the following section entitled "The Pure Land of the Ocean of Awakening" (*Juehai jingtu* 覺海淨土), is that both of these pure lands represent intermediary goals on the path to full awakening, and manifest within minds of awakening that are still tainted, as we just now saw in the quotation given in the previous section. Thus, the final goal is a mind free of all distinctions, even between individual buddhas and their lands, in the Great Ocean of Awakening. As way-stations on the path to final realization, Maitreya's Inner Court and Amitābha's Pure Land are of identical value.

The Importance of Scriptural Support

The translation of Taixu's Essay that appears in Part II comprises about 30,900 words. Within it, Taixu inserted eight lengthy citations from Buddhist sūtras and one Daoist source that, added together, are 20,295 words in length. In other words, direct quotations from scriptures make up about two-thirds of the overall text. In some places, Taixu does not insert the quotations in order to justify or illustrate a point he wishes to make. Instead, they stand on their own without comment to make his point for him, as when he compares the two Buddhist goals of rebirth in the Tuṣita Heaven and in the Pure Land of Amitābha. After noting that practices leading to rebirth as a human being on Earth or in Uttarakuru provide only temporary and incomplete relief from life's frustration and pain, he introduces the solution attained by rebirth in buddha-lands by saying "One can examine the holy teachings for their testimony" (Taixu 1956, 24:405). The sutra citations follow, the first on Maitreya's abode in the Tuṣita Heaven from T.452 and the second on Amitābha's Land of Bliss from T.366, both without any additional introduction or commentary. It thus appears that for Taixu, Buddhist sutras by themselves provided sufficient warrant to support his ideas.

Thus, as we conclude this introductory study and turn to the translation itself, I would advise the reader not to skip past the sutra quotations in the belief that only the portions of the Essay that Taixu composed convey his thoughts. Because Taixu embeds his own comments within some of the citations, but more importantly because he himself considered them integral to the Essay's message, the reader should read through them all in sequence. Only then can one know what Taixu wanted his readers to see and can thus discern the kind of modernizing project he wished to pursue.

Part Two

The Translation

6

The Translation: On the Establishment of the Pure Land in the Human Realm

(Jianshe renjian jingtu lun 建設人間淨土論)

By Master Taixu 太虛大師 (1890–1947)

Note: the numbers in parentheses reflect the pagination of the Chinese version found in volume 24 of the *Collected Works*.

Section 1: Where Humanity's Hope Lies (*Rensheng yuanwang zhi suozai* 人生願望之所在)

(356) What aspirations do we and all other sentient beings have by nature? There are innumerable schools of thought about this, but when one gets down to the sources, they reduce to two. The first is the need to secure our lives and requisites, and the Buddha said that only those in Uttarakuru do this to their satisfaction. Second, we wish to have immortality and bliss, and the Buddha said this need can be satisfied only in the Pure Land of Amitāyus. Let us speak first about securing life and property.

The "proper recompense" (*zheng bao* 正報) of human life refers to one's body and lifespan; the "dependent recompense" (*yi bao* 依報) of one's body and lifespan refers to one's possessions. Nothing beyond these is of any use. Now "body and lifespan" are nothing other than the ongoing fruits of karma in the storehouse consciousness (*yishou shi* 異熟識) along with the body with its senses. "Possessions" are things that extend and nourish the sense-consciousnesses to form the objects of the container-world. Thus, the delusions of worldlings in not knowing ultimate reality and their evolving consciousnesses are nothing but delusions within these [i.e., proper and dependent recompense]; a Tathāgata's awakening to discriminating cognition and inconceivable wisdom is likewise just awakening within these. Delusion and awakening may be different, but that upon which they depend is not two. No wonder that at the bottom of people's hearts the most basic aspiration is just to secure their lives and possessions! They seek to have all necessary possessions so that their lives may be free from worry. In order to extend their lives and pass it on to children and grandchildren, they protect their property by establishing households and countries. Unending complications arise from this. They go on to limitless future rebirths and all kinds of war and strife arise. Their very efforts to secure their lives and property become the very means by which life and property are lost.

At present, how are both "going white" (*baihua* 白化) in imperialist wars and "going red" (*chihua* 赤化) in class struggle not directed toward the securing of life and property, and yet how do their effects not threaten the loss of life and property![1] This is why we Buddhists grieve at their topsy-turvy distress and talk [instead] about the Ten Virtues whose karma resonates with the northern human realm of Uttarakuru. (357) The "Sumeru"[2] about which the Buddha spoke is just a general name for a solar system. Within this solar system, the human realm occupies four continents, of which the earth sits in the southern [continent] named Jambudvīpa. With regard to Uttarakuru, it is as the *Foshuo qishi yinben jing* 佛說起世因本經—as translated by Dharmagupta and others in the Sui dynasty in ten fascicles in the first "*Wu*" character case (*Dazang ezi han yi* 大藏惡字函一) of the scriptures—says in the second chapter [entitled] "On the Continent of Uttarakuru" (*Yudanyuezhou pin* 鬱單越洲品):[3]

> "O monks! The continent of Uttarakuru has mountains without number. Within all of its mountains, there are various kinds of trees. These trees are dense and lush, and emit various kinds of fragrances that permeate everywhere. Various

---

[1] As noted in Chapter 2, Taixu's associates and the wider public often voiced concerns about the country "going red" (*chihua* 赤化) in the 1910s and 1920s. However, the phrase had no precise definition and served as a floating signifier for views and actions its users deemed too revolutionary and leftist. The term Taixu uses to oppose it, "going white" (*baihua* 白化), is not similarly attested and may be Taixu's own invention, though the color white did often appear in opposition to the color red, as when writers spoke about a political party as the "white party" (*baidang* 白黨; see Wang 2010). In this Essay, Taixu makes his referents clear when he associates "going white" with imperialism and "going red" with the Marxist idea of class struggle.
[2] In traditional Buddhist cosmology, Sumeru is a vast mountain standing at the center of the cosmos, around which radiate the four continents which humans and animals inhabit. Uttarakuru is one of these continents. The hells are below it, while the gods (*devas*) live at its summit.
[3] Taixu says that this passage comes from the Dharmagupta translation of this sutra (T.25), but in fact he is quoting the Jñānagupta translation, also done in the Sui dynasty (T.24). The passage runs from T01n0024_p0314a11 to 317a16, and he does not reproduce it with complete accuracy. He inserted his own comments at various points, separated from the sutra text by a long dash, and I have followed his format here.

kinds of herbs grow all around that continent, all of a deep purple hue. They turn around clockwise with no effort like the down of a peacock, and their aroma is like the aloe flower (Skt.: *vārṣika*) and they feel like the garment of *kācalindikāka* (*jiazhanliantijia* 迦旃連提迦). They are all uniformly four fingers in length, and they lay down when one sets one's foot down and rise up again when one lifts one's foot. Besides these, there are multicolored fruit trees bearing all kinds of stalks, leaves, flowers, and fruit. They give off various kinds of fragrances that permeate everywhere."—Note: Whenever the Buddha described a sense-domain, he began by talking about the earth and fields, trees, herbs, and flowers. Thus we know that the Buddha paid special attention to the life [spent] within a flower garden.—

"There is a variety of birds, each singing of itself with a voice harmonious and refined. Their voices are subtle and wondrous. Within all of the mountains there are various rivers scattering in a hundred different currents. They flow downward flat and smooth, neither slowly nor rapidly, and without any waves. The banks are not deep, but are level, shallow, and easy to ford. Their waters are limpid and clear, with multitudes of flowers covering them. They are half a *yojana* wide"—Note: a *yojana* is equal to the distance of a waystation (*zhanlu* 站路)—"and their waters flow everywhere. There are groves of various kinds on both banks of all the rivers, growing along the waterline, and the leaves reflect one another. There are various kinds of fragrant flowers, various kinds of assorted fruits, green grasses that fill the spaces everywhere, and a chorus of birds that sings in harmony. (358) There are also marvelous boats along the banks, magnificent in their several colors and each one lovely in its own way. There are [boats of] the seven precious gems: gold, silver, lapis lazuli, crystal, ruby, mother-of-pearl, and agate."—Note: Every Buddhist sutra inclines to [depicting] trees that make music and flowers and birds that preach the dharma to address human beings who prize fragrance, form, and music above all. One could thus say these create the most perfect environment.—

O monks! The ground in the continent of Uttarakuru is flat and even, without any thorns or brambles, deep ravines, dense forests, pits, middens, or the impurities of excrement and filth. Its rocks and gravel are of pure gold and silver. It is neither cold nor hot, the seasons all being moderate. The ground is always smooth and covered with green grass, the branches and leaves of all its variegated trees are always splendid, its flowers and fruits are always in season.

O monks! There is a forest in that continent of Uttarakuru called "Peaceful Abiding" (*Anzhu* 安住),—Note: That is to say, only beings whose minds are at peace have the good fortune to live in this place—whose trees are all six *krośa* (*julushe* 拘盧奢) in height—a *krośa* is five *li* 里—with leaves heavy and dense enough that each touches its neighbors like a thatched roof so that no rain gets through. All the people there live beneath these trees.—Note: The book *Looking Backward, 2000-1887*[4] [by Edward Bellamy] advocates that there be a common covering over cities that would keep out the rain but let the breezes through. These trees are very similar in function—There are all kinds of fragrant trees also six *krośa* in height, or perhaps five *krośa*, or four, or three, or two, or one *krośa*, with the smallest being half a *krośa* high. All (359) bear various kinds of branches, leaves, flowers, and fruits. Upon all these trees wafts whatever kind of aromatic air that the heart desires.

There are also cottonwood trees (Skt. *karpāsa*) six *krośa* in height, on to five, or four, or three, or two, or one *krośa*, the smallest being likewise half a *krośa*. All have various kinds of branches, leaves, flowers, and fruits. From alongside these fruits, various kinds of garments spontaneously emerge suspended among the trees.

There are also trees featuring various kinds of jeweled garlands six *krośa* in height, on to five, or four, or three, or two, or one *krośa*, the smallest being likewise half a *krośa*. These also have various kinds of branches, leaves, flowers, and fruits. From alongside these fruits emerge various jeweled garlands hanging down as the heart desires.

There are also trees of adornments for the hair, these trees being six *krośa* in height, on to five, or four, or three, or two, or one *krośa*, the smallest being likewise half a *krośa*. They also have various kinds of branches, leaves, flowers, and fruits. From alongside these fruits emerge various kinds of hair ornaments suspended from the trees as the heart desires.

There are also trees bearing dishes—Note: that is, the devices and technologies of today—These trees are also six *krośa* in height, on to five, or four, or three, or two, or one *krośa*, the smallest being likewise half a *krośa*. They also bear various kinds of branches, leaves, flowers, and fruit, and from alongside these fruits emerge various forms of dishes as the heart desires.

There are various kinds of dishes hanging from these trees. There are also trees with many and varied kinds of assorted fruits—Note: various kinds of mechanical tubes—These trees are also six *krośa* in height, on to five, or four, or three, or two, or one *krośa*, the smallest being likewise half a *krośa*. They also bear various kinds of branches, leaves, flowers, and fruit, and from alongside these fruits emerge many various kinds of fruits as the heart desires on these trees.

---

[4] The Chinese text has 百年後新社會. A quick investigation indicates that he might be referring to a 1904 Japanese translation (*Hyakunengo no shinshakai* 百年後の新社會, Tokyo: 平民社 Heiminsha, Meiji 37 [1904]) of this book by Edward O. Bellamy, a nineteenth-century socialist writer and speaker.

Again, there are music trees. These trees are also six *krośa* in height, on to five, or four, or three, or two, or one *krośa*, the smallest being likewise half a *krośa*. They also bear various kinds of branches, leaves, flowers, and fruit, and from alongside these fruits emerge various kinds of musical instruments as the heart desires—Note: such as automated music boxes (*bayinhe* 八音盒)—suspended among the branches.

The land also spontaneously produces non-glutinous grains without the need for sowing. It is fresh, clean, and pure white in color and has no husk. Whenever one wishes to cook, (360) there are other fruits that are called *dunchi* (敦持) which may be used as cooking vessels with fire produced by rubies [placed underneath] rather than by firewood or charcoal. These produce flames of themselves.—Note: these are clearly modern electric, coal, or gas stoves—These will cook whatever food and drink one desires. As soon as the food is cooked, the ruby flames go out.—Note: This clearly says "dish-producing trees" and "ruby flames" so that one knows it [appears] by the Buddha's supernatural powers, [but] one can also plainly see today's mechanized world. In their massive form one can see today's mechanized factories, and the branches are just the conduits. People generally take [talk of] worlds like this where material culture is perfect as empty prattle. How wrong they are!—

O monks! Uttarakuru is surrounded on [all] four sides by the water of four lakes. All the lakes are called Anavatapta, and all are fifty *yojanas* across. Their waters are cool and gentle, sweet and light, clean and fragrant and without any impurity. They are surrounded by sevenfold ramparts, sevenfold steps, and sevenfold railings; seven nets laden with bells are suspended around them. They are also surrounded by seven rows of trees hung with many kinds of netting of manifold delightful colors made from the seven precious gems: gold, silver, lapis lazuli, crystal, ruby, coral, and cornelian. The four sides of each one of the ponds has a set of steps, and each and every set of steps is likewise made of these seven precious substances whose various colors are intricately woven together.

They are also possessed of all the flowers: the blue lotus (*utpala*), the red lotus (*padma*), the white budding lotus (*kumuda*), and the white lotus (*puṇḍarīka*) of blue-green, yellow, red, white, and light blue. Each flower is as big as a wagon wheel; their fragrance permeates the air with the greatest subtlety. Their roots are also as big around as a wagon wheel and when broken open, a juice the color of milk comes forth whose flavor is like honey.

The four sides of each of these Anavatapta-lakes are fed by a great river one *yojana* wide covered in a variety of flowers. Their water flows flat and even, in a straight path (361) with no bends, neither swiftly nor slowly, disturbed by neither waves nor rapids. Their banks are not high, but even, shallow, and easy to enter. On either bank of these rivers stand groves of various kinds whose branches cover one another and emit marvelous sounds. Various kinds of grasses grow by their sides, green in color and very soft, gently turning rightward. To be brief, we may skip to their height being a uniform four fingers. When one steps down on them, they go down too, and bounce back when one lifts one's foot. [These groves] also have all kinds of birds emitting a variety of sounds. On the two banks of those rivers there are also boats of various colors that one may enjoy, skipping ahead to[5] made of the seven precious substances: mother-of-pearl, agate, and so on. They are soft to the touch like a garment of *kācalindikāka*.

O monks! In Uttarakuru, dense clouds arise from these Anavatapta-lakes in the middle of every night and permeate all over. Once they have completely covered all of Uttarakuru and its mountains and seas, then it rains the waters of eight virtues like milk, reaching a depth of four fingers. It soaks the ground wherever it falls and does not run off in streams.—Note: this indicates underground waterways—While it is still the middle of the night, the rain stops and the clouds depart, leaving everything clean and pure. A wind arises from the sea and blows this sweet rain, fresh and gentle and bringing ease and pleasure to whatever it touches, over all of that continent of Uttarakuru, putting everything aright and making the *snigdha*-grass ever more luxuriant. It is as when a skilled hairdresser and her assistants, having styled the hair, then sprinkle it with water. Having been sprinkled, the hair becomes lustrous and bright. O monks! The ground of that continent of Uttarakuru is always moist, pleasant, and has a sheen as if people had spread fine butter upon it.

O monks! The continent of Uttarakuru also has a lake called Sudarśana (*Shanxian* 善現). Its water spans 100 *yojanas* across, and is cool, gentle, (362) pure, and free of pollution, with steps of the seven precious substances, skipping ahead to lotus roots as sweet as honey.—Note: The word "Sudarśana" indicates that the nature of the humans in this world is wondrous and fine (*shanmiao* 善妙), and this world appears (*xian* 現) in accordance. That is, strife and murder do not appear. [The text] below seems to have this meaning.—

O monks! To the east of Lake Sudarśana lies a garden, also called Sudarśana. This garden measures 100 *yojanas* in length and breadth and has seven rows of balustrade, seven layers of netting, and seven rows of trees within each layer of netting. These surround it on all sides and are of various pleasing colors, skipping ahead to all made of the seven precious substances: mother-of-pearl, agate, and so on. Every side [of the garden] has a gate. All are capable of holding off an

---

[5] There are elisions in the text of the sutra itself represented by the characters *naizhi* 乃至 ("skipping ahead to"), *lüeshuo* 略說 ("abbreviating"), or *naizhi lüeshuo* 乃至略說 ("skipping ahead for brevity to").

enemy, and are of various pleasing colors: gold, silver, lapis lazuli, coral, ruby, mother-of-pearl, and agate.—Note: In the World of Great Unity (*Datongshi* 大同世) silver is discarded and gold is relinquished. The ground is of gold of equal value, and so it is used to build walls, just as we use earth [for this].—

O monks! That garden Sudarśana is perfectly level and splendid, having no thorns or brambles, no hills, no holes or pits, no hard stones, no rubble, and no middens or any other kind of defilement.—Note: that is, they use a flushing mechanism to remove excrement—There are only different adornments of gold, silver, and so on. The seasons are all moderate, neither cold nor hot, and there are always springs flowing.—Note: running water—The four sides are replete with trees of numerous splendors. When their flowers bloom and fruits ripen, there are various scents that waft on the breeze and perfume [everything].

Again, there is a variety of different kinds of birds in profusion always emitting marvelous sounds that are harmonious and elegant, clear and unhurried. There is a kind of grass, blue-green in color that turns and twists to the right, soft and fine like peacock feathers, producing a delicate scent like aloe. Touching it is like touching a garment made of *kācalindikāka*. When one treads on it, it rises and falls along with the foot. There are also all kinds of trees, each having its own variety of root, trunk, flowers, leaves, and fruit, each emitting all kinds of scent to perfume everything around.

(363) O monks! Within that garden Sudarśana there is a forest called "Peaceful Abode" (*Anzhu* 安住),—Note: [Because] only people of peace and humanity may dwell there—whose trees grow to a height of six *krośa*. Their leaves are thick and heavy-spread so that rain cannot leak through. Moreover, they are arrayed in tight ranks as on a thatched roof, so that all the people may take shelter beneath them. There are also incense trees, cotton trees (*karpāsa*), necklace trees, hair-adornment trees, dish-producing trees, fruit trees, as well as trees that spontaneously produce cooked grains that are clean, pure, and fine.

O monks! That garden Sudarśana has no proprietor (*wo* 我) and no ruler; furthermore, it needs no protection.—Note: [The word] "protection" refers to soldiers and police. The World of Great Unity can dispense with them—When the people of Uttarakuru wish to enter that garden, then they go and disport themselves freely and enjoy all its pleasures. They go through its four gates as they will. Having entered that garden, they sport and play and bathe, taking pleasure to their hearts' content. If they wish to leave, they leave. If they wish to stay, they stay. They are free to follow their hearts.

O monks! To the south of Lake Sudarśana there is another garden for the use of the people of Uttarakuru. Its name is Universal Wisdom (*Puxian* 普賢).—Note: "Universal wisdom" is a characteristic among people found in Yao, Shun, immortals, and the Buddha. Their natures are all of universal wisdom.—This garden is 100 *yojanas* in length and breadth, (364) with seven rows of balustrades all around it, skipping ahead to [the trees that bear] cooked grains, clean, pure, and fine. O monks! This garden Universal Wisdom also has no owner or guardian,—One can see it dispenses with soldiers and police, and is governed like the [World of] Great Unity—and when the people of Uttarakuru wish to enter the garden Universal Wisdom to bathe, play, or enjoy its pleasures, then they enter through the four gates according to their wishes to bathe, play, and enjoy its pleasures. When they have disported themselves and wish to leave, then they leave. If they wish to stay, they stay.

O monks! To the west of Lake Sudarśana there is another garden for the use of the people of Uttarakuru. Its name is Virtue Flower (*Shanhua* 善華).—That is to say, the flower of the virtuous mind opens—This garden is one hundred *yojanas* in length and breadth, with seven balustrades encircling it, skipping ahead for brevity to it is just like the [eastern] garden Sudarśana without the slightest difference. It also has no owner or guardian,—Refer to what was said before about soldiers and police—and when the people of Uttarakuru wish to enter the garden Virtuous Flower to bathe, play, or enjoy its pleasures, then they enter through the four gates according to their wishes to bathe, play, and enjoy its pleasures. When they have disported themselves and wish to leave, then they leave. If they wish to stay, they stay.

O monks! To the north of Lake Sudarśana there is another garden for the use of the people of Uttarakuru. Its name is "Virtuous Pleasure" (*Shanle* 善樂).— It has no sadness, only joy, great joy—Its length and breadth equal exactly one hundred *yojanas*, skipping ahead to it has no owner or guardian, and when the people of Uttarakuru wish to enter the garden Virtuous Pleasure to bathe, play, or enjoy its pleasures, then they enter through the four gates according to their wishes to bathe, play, and enjoy its pleasures. When they have disported themselves and wish to leave, then they leave. If they wish to stay, they stay. We might say in summary that it is like the [eastern] garden Sudarśana [described] above.

O monks! To the east of Lake Sudarśana in the interval where it meets the garden Sudarśana there is a river for the sake of the people of Uttarakuru whose name is "Easily Entered Path"—that is to say, it is easy for the people to enter the path of virtue—which gradually winds its way without any pools or ripples—the people are without defilements—neither slow nor fast. Various flowers cover it all over, and it is two and a half *yojanas* in width.

O monks! On both sides of this river Easily Entered Path there are various and sundry trees covered in radiant branches and leaves that give off various and sundry fragrances that pervade everywhere. Various types of grasses grow there, skipping ahead for brevity to upon touching them they are soft like garments of *kācalindikāka*. It grows evenly to four fingers, and when a foot treads upon it, it is pressed down and rises up along with the foot, sometimes standing up, sometimes bent down. Also, there is a variety of trees bearing multicolored fruit all with plenty of branches, leaves, flowers, and fruits. They also give off various and sundry fragrances that pervade everywhere, and various and sundry different birds all sing (365) harmoniously together. On the two banks of this river are all the wondrous pleasure-boats of various colors that are made of the seven precious substances: gold, silver, lapis lazuli, crystal, rubies, mother-of-pearl, and agate, all splendidly arrayed.— All of this is repeated to explain that the human mind appears virtuous [*shanxian* 善現, or Sudarśana], the flower of the human mind opens, and the path of virtue is easy to enter. The mind is without ripples. This means both the nature of the people and their environment are constructed at the same time.—

O monks! To the south of Lake Sudarśana there is a great river named "Essence of Virtue" (*Shanti* 善體) for the sake of the people of Uttarakuru.—It has virtue as its essence; there is nothing evil—It winds its way down, skipping ahead for brevity to just like the river Easily Entered Path. The various and sundry trees in this place are different from those of that [other place]; skipping ahead to boats of many colors made [of the precious substances], and [trees with leaves] as soft as garments made of *kācalindikāka*.

O monks! To the west of Lake Sudarśana there is a great river named "Equal Vehicles" (*Dengche* 等車).—This means equality. The *Lotus Sutra* speaks of equality with the Great Vehicle as one attains buddhahood [in all of them]—, skipping ahead for brevity to it winds its way down.

O monks! To the north of Lake Sudarśana there is a great river named "Power Sovereign" (*Weizhu* 威主) for the sake of the people of Uttarakuru—The people are all sovereign and free—winding its way down. Skipping ahead for brevity to on its two banks are boats, splendid with the seven precious materials, as soft as garments made of *kācalindikāka*.

In the midst of this is an *udāna-gāthā*:

Sudarśana [or "Well-Appearing"], Samantabhadra [or "Universal Compassion"] and the rest

Flower of Virtue along with Joy and Pleasure,

The rivers Easily Entered along with Essence of Virtue,

Equal Vehicles and Power Sovereign.

—If one wishes to obtain joy and pleasure, one must first pay the price of virtue and happiness. —

O monks! When the people of Uttarakuru wish to bathe or sport or enjoy all the pleasures in the river Easily Entered Path, or the rivers Essence of Virtue, Equal Vehicles, or Power Sovereign, they have only to come to the twin banks of those rivers. They remove their clothes, place themselves beside the banks, and each sits down in a boat. When the boat arrives (366) in the middle of the water, then they bathe themselves, sport and play, and enjoy its pleasures. Once they are done bathing, then they follow along behind whichever person went prior to them, and when they have put on that person's clothes, then they leave. They do not seek to put back on the clothes they originally came in.—Nowadays, when people go into the hospital, none of them keeps on their original clothing. In the future, the world of the Great Unity will be like this.—And why? The people of Uttarakuru have [no concept of] "me" or "mine," and thus they are not possessive. Also, when they congregate under the fragrant trees, once they arrive under a tree, the tree spontaneously lowers its branches to impart its various aromas to all of them.—This is very clearly an automated perfume device—They gather [the branches] into their own hands. When the people have taken these various perfumes and applied them on their bodies, then they go and gather at the cotton trees—This is an automated wardrobe—and when they have arrived, then as before the trees bend down and produce various and sundry clothes, which the people gather with their hands. When the people have picked the finest raiment from these trees, then they put them on and go. They proceed further to the foot of the trees of adornment. Once they have arrived, the adornment trees likewise lower their branches—This is an automated makeup kit—which give forth various kinds of fine adornments for all those people, which they gather into their hands. The people select from those trees various kinds of adornments, and when they have put them on, then they go to the foot of the hair adornment trees. When they have arrived at these trees, then the hair adornment trees spontaneously lower their branches for those people and give forth various kinds of jeweled hairpieces, which the people take into their hands. They select fine ornaments from the trees, and when they have placed them on their heads, then they proceed on to gather at the dish-giving trees. Having arrived at the trees, dishes spontaneously bend down from the branches and leaves for them to gather in their hands according to their wishes. When they have selected their dishes, they hold the assembled fruits of these trees. At that time the fruits also bend low for these people (367) and produce various and sundry fruits of marvelous sweetness—An edible fruit machine—which they gather in their hands. These people gather ripe fruit from these trees as their hearts desire and they eat them as they wish. They might squeeze some of them for their juice, filling a dish and drinking it,—A juice machine—and when their meal is over, they return to the grove of music.—a music machine—Once there, then the branches of all the music trees bend low for these people, and bestow musical instruments on them which they gather in their hands. Each selects the instrument they want from the trees, all of which are of particularly lovely form and produce harmonious and elegant music. Once they have them in their hands, then they roam east and play west. If they want to play [the instruments] then they play; if they want to dance, they dance; if they want to sing, they sing. Following their mood, they enjoy the pleasures deriving from the music. When they are done, then they all do as they please. They may leave, or they may stay.—Note: This passage is very clear. It indicates that in the Great Unity the parks will be for public use and all requisites will be manufactured. People today already have use of them, but the pity is that they cannot each take what they need because their good nature has not yet manifested.—

O monks! The people of Uttarakuru all have sky-blue hair eight fingers in length. All the people are of the same kind, the same form, the same color. There are no other forms or colors by which to differentiate them.—This is extremely important. The races of humans evolved, and the inferior races were eliminated. These days everyone is discussing eugenics just for this purpose.—

O monks! Everyone in Uttarakuru has clothing. No one goes naked or only half-clothed. They are all equally related, and there are none that are either too intimate or too distant. Their teeth are all even and close with no gaps and no insufficiency. They are beautiful, wonderful, pure, and clean, and are as white as [white] jade and fresh, bright, and attractive.

O monks! When the people of Uttarakuru are hungry or thirsty and need drink or food, they gather it themselves without plowing or sowing: naturally polished rice, pure, fresh, and white (368) without any chaff. Once they have gathered it they spoon it out amidst the fruits in their dishes, after which they take the fire-pearls which they place beneath the dishes. [By] the power of living beings' good fortune—The achievement of education along with the power of cognition—the fire-pearls then suddenly produce flames, and when the food and drink are cooked, the flames extinguish themselves. When those people have obtained their food and wish to eat, they set out dishes and utensils, go to their seats and sit. If at that time people come from the four directions and wish to eat together—In ancient Sparta the people and kings would enter the dining hall together. In the future we should also do away with private kitchens, as when Russell spoke of common dormitories and refectories and Kropotkin spoke of common kitchens—they set out [more] food to eat. The food is never exhausted skipping ahead to the food and servings are never finished; the food dishes are always full to overflowing. That which those people eat is free from chaff and husks and is naturally white, polished rice. When the food is ready, it is clean, pure, and fragrant, possessed of all the flavors. There is no need for soup or [other] delicacies. The form and color of the food are like the flavors of heavenly ambrosia and is fresh, white, and bright as a bouquet. When they are done eating, they feel satisfied and they lack nothing. Tranquil, they do not change; they neither age nor alter [their appearance]. This food skipping ahead to nourishes and benefits those people in color, strength, peace, and eloquence is sufficient.

O monks! When the people of Uttarakuru experience the desires of men for women, then he turns his gaze upon the woman he desires, who will then know of it and follow him. They will then resort to the foot of a tree, and if the woman he has brought turns out to be his mother, his aunt, his sister, or another relative, then the branches will remain as they were without bending down for them, the leaves will turn yellow according to the season and fall off, they will not knit together to form a mat, nor will they produce flowers and fruits, nor will they (369) form a bed for them to lie upon. [Otherwise] they will go together beneath the tree and do as they wish, enjoying great pleasure.—This proves even more that these trees are [part of] a public park in a great power plant. In the World of Great Unity, the people will revert to the times before [sage-emperor] Fuxi, when there were no family names and people kept track of their blood-lines by tattooing their bodies with the [signs of] the Celestial Stems and Terrestrial Branches.—

O monks! The people of Uttarakuru reside in their mothers' wombs for just seven days; on the eighth they are born. After birth, whether the [babies] are male or female, their mothers take them to the middle of a crossroads and leave them there.—This clearly states that males and females all receive public support.— People come there from the east, west, south, and north, and when they see these boys and girls, they give rise to feelings of affection. In order to nourish them, they each put a finger into [the babies'] mouths, and superior milk and sweet milk spontaneously flow from their fingertips.—This is just like the modern use of mechanized nipples.—When they have drunk, then these boys and girls receive all they need for life. They drink milk in this manner for seven days, after which all these boys' and girls' bodies mature uniformly, showing no difference from those of their elders. The men then follow after the men and the women follow after the women, departing along with their companions.—People follow the great masses, and all under Heaven truly becomes one household.—

O monks! The people of Uttarakuru have a set lifespan; there is no premature death. When their life is up, they all go to a superior rebirth. By what causes and conditions do all the people of Uttarakuru attain this set lifespan and go to a superior rebirth? O monks! In this world there are people whose principal practices are killing, stealing, licentiousness, idle babble, double-talk, evil speech, lascivious talk, greed, anger, or heretical views. By these causes and conditions, when their bodies decay and their lives end, they fall into the evil (370) paths, taking birth in a hell-realm. Perhaps there are others who have not killed beings, stolen others' property, committed sexual improprieties, engaged in idle babble, double-talk, evil speech, or lascivious talk, are not greedy or angry, and hold no heretical views. By these causes and conditions, when their bodies decay and their lives end, they go toward the better paths and take birth among humans or *devas*. By what causes and conditions does one tend toward a lower rebirth? By killing and heretical views. By what causes and conditions does one tend toward a higher rebirth? By not killing and holding correct views.

Perhaps there are others who reflect thus: "I should practice the Ten Virtues in the present, and by means of these causes and conditions, when my body decays I will be able to attain rebirth in Uttarakuru.—This says that people can now put the Ten Virtues into practice, and [this world would] turn into Uttarakuru—Having been born there, I will abide for a thousand years, no more and no less." Since those people have set forth this aspiration and practiced the Ten Virtues, when their bodies decay they attain birth in Uttarakuru; they are born in that place and receive a fixed lifespan of one thousand years, no more and no less. O monks! By means of such causes and conditions do the people of Uttarakuru receive a fixed lifespan.

O monks! By what causes and conditions does one attain a higher rebirth? O monks! The people of Jambudvīpa receive the karma of the Ten Virtues from another place, so when their lives end they attain rebirth in Uttarakuru. By their past practice of the Ten Virtues and by conducting themselves according to the dharma while in Uttarakuru, when their bodies decay and their lives end, the people of Uttarakuru go to a higher birth in good places [like] the *deva*-realms. O monks! By such causes and conditions do the people of Uttarakuru go to a higher rebirth in a superior place.

O monks! When the people of Uttarakuru reach the end and abandon their lives, there is not one person who grieves or cries over their loss. They merely carry the body to a crossroads, leave it there, and go. O monks! In Uttarakuru there is such a law that if there are beings whose lifespans have been exhausted, then there is a bird called the Uccaṁgama (371)—The [people of the] Sui [dynasty] called this a high death—that flies swiftly from the mountains and takes hold of the deceased person's hair. Carrying the corpse away it casts it into the waters of other continents.—This is another sort of flying machine. In the future we will use airships to dispose of corpses.—And why? The people of Uttarakuru practice purity. Because they delight in purity and cleanliness and wish for happiness, they do not allow the breezes to blow the foul odors of decay to them.

O monks! When the people of Uttarakuru need to defecate or urinate, the earth opens up for them, and when they are done, the earth closes back up.—This would be a flush toilet—. And why? Because the people of Uttarakuru delight in purity and happiness.

Again, under what causes and conditions does that place go under the name "Uttarakuru"? O monks! Compared to the other three continents under the four heavens, Uttarakuru is the best, the most wondrous, the highest, the most excellent. That is why it is called "Uttarakuru."—"Uttarakuru" is translated as "Most Excellent." The words "Fortune," "Virtue," and "Excellence of Karma" also get at this.

The above words on Uttarakuru indicate that it is not above the heavens nor is it a Pure Land lying in some other place, but is actually an abode for human beings within this solar system. This particular solar system has four habitations for human beings; this one is the best exemplar among them. Since it is the best example of a human domain within this solar system, it is one that we human beings may reach. We observe that in this model human realm, blessings fill the entire continent, so all requisites are taken care of. Lifespans are fixed at 1,000 years, so the security of one's life is worry-free. We can say that it fulfills all our human aspirations for "security of life and possessions." We only need to find a way to attain the causes of its excellent results, namely the practice of the Ten Virtues. (372) Thus, we know that if now we want to fulfill our desires for security of life and possessions, then we should counsel only the practice of the Ten Virtues as the way to get them. If we could put this belief in the way of Uttarakuru into practice throughout Jambudvīpa (i.e., this planet Earth), then Jambudvīpa could become like Uttarakuru. Get busy! Tell everyone to practice the Ten Virtues assiduously! Get busy! Tell everyone to practice the Ten Virtues assiduously!

Next, we will talk about attaining eternal life in the [Land of] Utmost Bliss: Even though one attains security of life and requisites in Uttarakuru, one's lifespan is still limited to 1,000 years. When that time is up, then one dies with no prospect of immortality. Blessings fill the entire continent, but only within a limited range, and so it does not reach the fullest extent of bliss. Because one's lifespan does not last forever, and we are pleased [only] when we have the full extent of the things we need, our basic desires go unfulfilled. Because of this, there is the Pure Land of the Buddha Amitāyus of which the Buddha spoke, as stated in the *Larger Sukhāvatī-vyūha-sūtra*:[6]

---

[6] This long quotation from the *Larger Sukhāvatī-vyūha sūtra* runs from T12n0360_p0270a07 to 272c10. See also Inagaki and Stewart (2003, 24–36). I have translated this anew because Taixu does not use the familiar Taishō version of the text and he skips over various parts.

"The seven jewels (gold, silver, beryl, coral, amber, mother-of-pearl, and agate) come together spontaneously to form the earth of his buddha-land, so vast and sprawling that its farthest bounds admit of no limit. Their features combine on every side and intermingle in light that is fiery, dazzling, and wondrous in its beauty. Its purity and magnificence are unrivalled among all the worlds of the ten directions. They are the finest among gems, like the jewels of the sixth *deva*-heaven. Furthermore, his buddha-land has no Mount Sumeru or any of the other mountains that encircle it, nor does it have any great oceans, small seas, streams and channels, or wells and valleys. By the power of the Buddha, one can see [such things] if one wishes. It also lacks the difficult paths of rebirth in hell or as hungry ghosts or animals. In addition, it is without the four seasons: spring, summer, fall, and winter, and it is neither cold nor hot. (373) It is always suitable."

Then Ānanda asked the Buddha, "World-honored one! If that land has no Mount Sumeru, then what supports its [Heaven of the] Four *Deva* Kings and its Heaven of the Thirty-three?" The Buddha said to Ānanda, "What supports the third heaven of Yāma on up to the highest Heaven of the Form Realm?" Ānanda said to the Buddha, "Karmic retribution is inconceivable." The Buddha told Ānanda, "Karmic retribution is inconceivable, and all buddha-lands are inconceivable. The virtuous power of the merits of sentient beings abides on a ground of karma, and that is how they [exist without the support of a Mount Sumeru]." Ānanda said to the Buddha, "I have no doubts about this teaching, but I wished to remove these qualms for the sake of sentient beings in the future."

The Buddha said to Ānanda, "The majestic light of the Buddha Amitāyus is foremost; no other buddha's light can approach it. They might illuminate a hundred buddha-lands or a thousand buddha-lands. In brief, [the light of Amitāyus] illuminates buddha-lands to the east as numerous as the sands of the Ganges; the same goes for those to the south, west, north, the four intermediate points, and up and down. The light of some buddhas reaches to seven *chi* (尺), or to one *yojana*, or to two, three, four, or five *yojanas*, increasing in this way up to the point of illuminating one buddha-land. This is why Amitāyus is called Amitābha, the Buddha of Boundless Light, the Buddha of Unobstructed Light, the Buddha of Incomparable Light, the Buddha of the Blaze-King Light, the Buddha of Pure Light, the Buddha of the Light of Joy, the Buddha of Wisdom-Light, the Buddha of Uninterrupted Light, the Buddha of Light Difficult to Conceive, the Buddha of Unnamable Light, and the Buddha of Light Surpassing Sun and Moon. Those sentient beings who encounter his light find the three defilements eliminated, become pliant in body and thought, they leap and dance for joy and give rise to a virtuous mind. If they are in one of the places of the three extreme kinds of suffering and see his light, then they all receive respite and their afflictions will not return. At the end of their lives, they all gain liberation."

"The light of the Buddha Amitāyus (374) shines brilliantly, illuminating all of the buddha-lands of the ten directions; there is none that it does not reach. I am not the only one who gives praise to his light; all of the assemblies of buddhas, *śrāvakas*, *pratyekabuddhas*, and bodhisattvas join to sing its praises in the same way. If sentient beings hear of the majestic merit of his light and speak its praise day and night with a mind of continuous sincerity, then they can attain rebirth in his land according to their aspiration, and all the bodhisattvas and *śrāvakas* will join to sing their praises and glorify their merit. In the end they will attain buddhahood, and then all the buddhas and bodhisattvas of the ten directions will praise their light just as happens now."

The Buddha said, "Were I to praise the majestic, awesome, and wondrous light of Amitāyus day and night for a *kalpa*, I would not exhaust it."

The Buddha said to Ānanda, "Moreover, the lifespan of Amitāyus is incalculable. How can one fathom this? Let us suppose that all of the sentient beings from the ten directions attained a human rebirth and they all achieved the status of *śrāvaka* or *pratyekabuddha*. Then they all gathered and pondered together with one mind, exerting the power of their wisdom to its utmost to perform calculations for a hundred, a thousand, ten thousand *kalpas* in order to arrive at the length of his lifespan. They still could not reach its full extent. The lifespans of the *śrāvakas*, bodhisattvas, *devas*, and humans in his assembly are likewise incalculable, and not to be known by any kind of reckoning or simile."

"Again, the number of *śrāvakas* and bodhisattvas [in Sukhāvatī] is hard to measure and cannot be communicated. Their supernatural wisdom penetrates everywhere and they exercise their majestic power as they please. They can hold all the worlds in the palms of their hands. When that Buddha first convened his *śrāvaka*-assembly, their number was uncountable; same with his bodhisattvas. If [they all, like] Mahāmaudgalyāyana took a hundred, a thousand, ten thousand, a billion incalculable *nayutas* of *kalpas*, even until they reached final nirvana to calculate it together, they still could not fully fathom how great the number was. For comparison, suppose there were a man who split a hair into a hundred pieces, and with just one piece took a drop from the great ocean (375), boundless in depth and breadth. What do you think? Which is more, the drop of water or the great ocean?" Ānanda said to the Buddha, "The proportion of that drop of water to the great ocean cannot be known even by one with skill in astronomy, mathematics, rhetoric, or metaphor." The Buddha said to Ānanda, "Even if Mahāmaudgalyāyana counted for a hundred, a thousand, ten thousand, or a billion *nayutas* of *kalpas*, the number of *śrāvakas* and bodhisattvas in that first convocation [in Sukhāvatī] that could be known is like the drop of water, while the number that remained unknown would be like the water of the great ocean."

"Again, in that land trees of the seven jewels fill the domain all around: gold trees, silver trees, beryl trees, crystal trees, coral [trees], cornelian trees, and mother-of-pearl trees. Some trees combine two, three, up to all seven jewels. Some are gold trees with silver leaves, flowers, and fruit; some are silver trees with gold leaves, flowers, and fruit; some are beryl trees with crystal leaves, as are its flowers and fruits; some are crystal trees with beryl leaves, flowers, and fruits; some are coral trees with cornelian leaves, flowers, and fruits; some are cornelian trees with beryl leaves, flowers, and fruits; some are mother-of-pearl trees with all the other jewels as leaves, flowers, and fruits.

"There are jeweled trees with purple-gold roots, stalks of white silver, beryl branches, crystal twigs, coral leaves, cornelian flowers, and mother-of-pearl fruits. (*shi* 實). There are jeweled trees with beryl stalks, crystal branches, coral twigs, beryl leaves, mother-of-pearl flowers, and purple-gold fruits. There are jeweled trees with beryl roots, crystal stalks, coral branches, cornelian twigs, mother-of-pearl leaves, purple-gold flowers, and white silver fruits. There are jeweled trees with crystal roots, coral stalks, (376) cornelian branches, mother-of-pearl twigs, purple-gold leaves, white silver flowers, and beryl fruits. Some jeweled trees have roots of coral, cornelian stalks, mother-of-pearl branches, purple-gold twigs, white silver leaves, beryl flowers, and crystal fruits. Some jeweled trees have roots of cornelian, mother-of-pearl stalks, purple-gold branches, white silver twigs, beryl leaves, crystal flowers, and coral fruits. There are jeweled trees with mother-of-pearl roots, purple-gold stalks, white silver branches, beryl twigs, crystal leaves, coral flowers, and cornelian fruits. [The trees] stand in parallel rows, their trunks facing each other, their branches in symmetry, their leaves facing one another, every flower in perfect order, and their fruits well matched. Their glorious colors are brilliant; there is nothing better to see! When breezes waft through them they emit the five tones, the subtle and marvelous *gong* and *shang* in spontaneous harmony.

"Also, the Bodhi tree of the Buddha Amitāyus is four million *li* in height and five thousand *yojanas* around at its root. Its branches and leaves spread to two hundred thousand *li* in the four directions. It is made up of every kind of gem spontaneously combined, and is adorned by moon-glow *maṇi* gems and ocean-supporting wheel gems, the kings of all jewels. The spaces between its twigs are hung with various jewels of a hundred, a thousand, ten thousand colors from which blaze forth immeasurable light without bound. Nets of wondrous jewels surmount it, and all kinds of adornments appear as one wishes.

"When a gentle breeze arises, blowing through the branches of the jeweled trees, it produces innumerable wondrous dharma-sounds. The sound spreads to all the buddha-lands, and those who hear it attain a deep forbearance of dharmas and the stage of non-retrogression. They achieve the buddha-way, their ears remain clear and penetrating, and they meet with no suffering or anxiety. Their eyes will see its colors, their noses will know its fragrance, their mouths will taste its flavors, their bodies will touch its light, and their minds will attune to the Dharma. They will all achieve profound forbearance of dharmas and abide in the stage of non-retrogression. Until they attain the buddha-way (377), their six senses will be clear and penetrating and they will be free of anger or worry.

"O Ānanda! If the *devas* and humans of that land see this tree, they attain three kinds of dharma-forbearance: First, the forbearance through sound; second, the forbearance of pliancy; third, the forbearance of the unarisen [nature of] dharmas. All this is effected by the Buddha Amitāyus's numinous power, by the power of his originary vows, by his fulfillment of [those] vows, his clear vows, his firm vows, and his thoroughly complete vows."

The Buddha said to Ānanda, "A worldly monarch has a hundred thousand [kinds of] music. From the [realm of a] wheel-turning monarch up to the sixth *deva*-heaven, the music of each realm is superior by a thousand billion times [to that of the level just below]. The ten thousand [kinds of] music of the sixth *deva*-heaven is a hundred thousand billion times inferior to just one kind produced by the seven-jeweled trees in the land of Amitāyus, and they produce ten thousand kinds of music spontaneously. None of this music is lacking in the sound of the Dharma. These sounds are clear and serene, poignant and luminous, subtle and marvelous, harmonious and elegant. In all the worlds of the ten directions, this music is the most excellent.

"The lecture halls, *vihāras*, palaces, and towers are all adorned with the seven jewels that come together spontaneously. These are surmounted by nets of pearl, bright-moon *maṇi*, and various gems. Inside and out, to both right and left, there are bathing pools, some ten *yojanas*, some twenty *yojanas*, or thirty on up to a hundred *yojanas* in both width and depth. All are filled with limpid water of the eight excellent qualities, pure, fragrant, and clean, and with a taste like sweet nectar. The golden pools have beds of white-silver sand, and the white-silver pools have beds of golden sand. The crystal pools have beds of beryl sand, and the beryl pools have beds of crystal sand. The coral pools have beds of amber sand, and the amber pools have beds of coral sand. The mother-of-pearl pools have beds of agate sand, and the agate pools have beds of mother-of-pearl (378) sand. The white-jade pools have beds of purple-gold sand, and the purple-gold pools have beds of white-jade sand. They might have two kinds of jewel, or three, or up to all seven kinds of jewels combining to form them.

"By the banks of these pools, there are sandalwood trees whose outstretched flowers and leaves spread a fragrance that pervades everywhere. The surface of the water is covered by a profusion of heavenly lotuses of blue, pink, yellow, white, and various other colors. When all the assemblies of bodhisattvas and śrāvakas enter into the jeweled pools, then if they wish for the water to cover their feet, it covers their feet. If they want the water to come up to their knees, then it comes up to their knees. If they want the water to come up to their waists, then it comes up to their waists. If they want the water to come up to their necks, then it comes up to their necks. If they want it to shower their bodies, then it spontaneously showers their bodies. If they want the water to recede then straightaway, it recedes. The temperature is cold or warm just as they wish, opening up their spirits, gladdening their bodies, and ridding their minds of impurities. [The water] is clear, bright, and limpid, so pure that it is formless and the jeweled sand-beds reflect the light perfectly at any depth.

"The ripples ebb and flow, turning about and flowing into one another peacefully and gently, neither too slow nor too fast. The waves proclaim innumerable wonderful sounds in accordance with whatever one wishes to hear. Some might hear the sound 'Buddha,' some the sound 'dharma,' some the sound 'sangha.' Some will hear the sound 'serenity,' or the sound 'emptiness and no-self,' or the sound 'great compassion,' or the sounds 'perfection,' 'ten powers,' 'fearlessness,' or the sound of 'individual dharmas,' or the sound 'all supernatural powers,' or the sounds 'wisdom,' 'nonaction,' 'no arising or perishing,' 'forbearance of the unproduced,' and so on up to 'anointing with sweet dew,' and the sounds of all the marvelous dharmas. Such sounds as these bring limitless joy to whoever hears them. They accord with the teachings of purity, absence of desire, calm extinction, and reality. They accord with the Three Treasures, power that fears nothing, individual dharmas, and accord with supernatural powers, wisdom, and the cultivation of the way of bodhisattvas and śrāvakas. They separate one from even the names of the three paths of suffering, but are only sounds of spontaneous joy. For this reason the land is called Peace and Joy. Ānanda! (379) All who achieve rebirth in that buddha-land are replete with purified forms and sounds such as these, with the virtues of all the marvelous sounds and supernatural powers.

"The palaces in which they dwell, their clothing, food and drink, the wonderful flowers and incense, and the magnificent adornments they possess are like those that appear spontaneously in the sixth *deva*-heaven [of the desire realm]. Whenever they wish to eat, bowls and utensils made of the seven jewels appear before them. As they desire, bowls and utensils of gold, silver, beryl, cornelian, agate, coral, amber, true bright-moon pearl and such arrive spontaneously filled with drink and food of the hundred [good] flavors. Though they have this food, they do not actually eat it. Once they have seen its form and smelled its fragrance, it will be as if they had eaten and they naturally feel satisfied. Their minds and bodies relax and they experience no attachment to [good] tastes. When they are finished, everything magically vanishes, only to appear once again when the time comes. That buddha-land is pure and serene, marvelous and happy. It is second [only] to the path of unconditioned nirvana.

"All of the *śrāvakas*, bodhisattvas, and *devas* [there] possess lofty and brilliant wisdom and have thoroughly mastered the supernatural powers. They are all the same, without any distinction in form, but in conformity to other regions they bear the names *devas* and humans. Their appearance is elegant and upright, rarely found throughout the worlds. Their countenances are delicate and marvelous unlike [those of] *devas* and humans. They all receive spontaneous and vacuous bodies, limitless bodies."

The Buddha said to Ānanda, "Suppose there was an impoverished beggar next to a great monarch. Would they be comparable in appearance and form?"

Ānanda said to the Buddha, "Were such a man to stand next to a great monarch, his mean and repulsive appearance could not be compared [with the monarch's by saying it was] a hundred, a thousand, ten thousand, or one hundred million times worse."[7]

The Buddha said to Ānanda, "You have spoken rightly. Even though a great monarch is esteemed most highly among the people, and his appearance and form are august and upright, when compared with a great wheel-turning monarch, then he will appear as inferior as did the beggar next to a great monarch. The majestic appearance of a wheel-turning monarch (380) is especially wondrous, preeminent among all under heaven, but compared with the King of the Heaven of the Thirty-Three, then he also appears base and mean by ten thousand or a billion times. Now suppose you were to compare the King of [this] heaven with the King of the Sixth Heaven [of the Desire Realm]. He would be a hundred, a thousand, ten thousand, a billion times inferior. In comparison to the luminous forms and countenances of the bodhisattvas and *śrāvakas* of the land of Amitāyus Buddha, [the King of the Sixth Heaven] would be outmatched by a hundred, a thousand, ten thousand, a billion, or an incalculable number of times."

The Buddha said to Ānanda, "All the *devas* and humans in the land of Amitāyus are provided with clothing, drink, food, flowers, incense, adornments, silk coverings, pennants, and exquisite sounds. The houses, palaces, and pavilions in which they dwell are matched to their bodies in height and size. They might be made from one kind of jewel, two kinds, or even innumerable kinds of jewels just as they wish. They appear in accordance with their thoughts. In addition, wondrous cloth of the many kinds of jewels covers the ground upon which the *devas* and humans walk. Innumerable jeweled nets cover that buddha-land

---

[7] Taixu's citation omits a long stretch of Ānanda's response, found between T12n0360_p0271c13 and 271c26.

over, all magnificently adorned with gold thread, true pearls, and a hundred, a thousand assorted marvelous gems. Jeweled bells of luminous and radiant form hang from these on all four sides. They are beautiful to the extreme! When a delicate motion arises, it is temperate, neither cold nor hot, but [only] warm or cool. It is soft and gentle, not slow or fast. When it blows through the nets and the jeweled trees, it puts forth innumerable subtle dharma-sounds and permeates everywhere with scents of a myriad kinds of refined virtue. Impurities and evil habits cease to arise in those who hear them. When the breeze brushes upon their bodies, they all attain great joy, just as a monk who has achieved the *samādhi* of extinction.

"Also, when the breeze blows, flowers scatter, covering over that buddha-land. They fall according to their color and are not mixed. They are soft and lustrous and their fragrance is rich. When one steps on them, they press down four inches, and when one steps off, they recover their former height. When the flowers have served their purpose, they vanish into the ground, leaving it clear and pure without a trace. (381) The flowers scatter in the breeze in this way six times each day.

"Again, all kinds of jeweled lotuses encircle this world. Each one has a hundred, a thousand, a billion leaves, and their light glistens with innumerable colors. The green ones emit green light, the white ones white light, the dark, the yellow, the red, and the purple all emit forms of vibrant light, blazing forth brighter than the sun and moon. From each flower comes thirty-six hundred thousand billion rays of light. Thirty-six hundred thousand billion buddhas emerge from each ray of light, going into all the ten directions to preach the wondrous dharma. Each one of these buddhas establishes countless sentient beings in the proper buddha-way."

The Buddha said to Ānanda, "All sentient beings who attain rebirth in that buddha-land will dwell in the assembly of those settled in right *samādhi*. Why is this? Because the assemblies of heretics and of those not settled are not to be found in that buddha-land. All of the buddha-*tathāgatas* of the ten directions [as numerous as] the sands of the Ganges praise Amitāyus's inconceivable power and virtue. Any sentient being who hears his name with faith and joy even just once and sincerely dedicates their merit to the aspiration for birth in that land will instantly attain rebirth and the stage of non-retrogression. The only exceptions will be those who have committed the Five Heinous Deeds or slandered the true Dharma."

The Buddha said to Ānanda, "All of the *devas* and humans of the ten directions who aspire to rebirth in that land with sincere minds fall into three broad categories. Those of the highest category leave their homes, abandon desires, and become *śramaṇas*. They generate *bodhicitta*, focus their minds exclusively on the Buddha Amitāyus, cultivate all forms of merit, and aspire to rebirth in that land. When those in this class reach the end of their lives, Amitāyus and his retinue will appear before them and they will follow that Buddha to rebirth in his land. They will take birth by spontaneous transformation within a seven-jeweled flower, abide in the stage of non-retrogression, and have wisdom, courage, (382) supernatural power, and utter freedom. For this reason, Ānanda, if any beings wish to see Amitāyus in this life, they should generate unsurpassed *bodhicitta*, cultivate meritorious practices, and aspire to birth in that buddha-land!

"Those of the middle category include *devas* and humans of the worlds of the ten directions who aspire to rebirth in that land with sincere minds. Although they are unable to become *śramaṇas* or greatly cultivate merit, they should generate unsurpassed *bodhicitta*. They concentrate exclusively on the Buddha Amitāyus, cultivate some degree of virtue, observe the Eight Vows of Abstinence, construct *stūpas* and images, offer alms to the *śramaṇas*, hang banners, light lamps, scatter flowers, burn incense, and dedicate all the [resulting] merit to rebirth in that land. When they reach the ends of their lives, Amitāyus will appear as a transformation-body with all the brilliance and distinguishing marks of an actual buddha. With all his great assemblies, he will appear before these people and they will immediately follow this transformation-buddha to rebirth in his land, there to abide in the stage of non-retrogression. Their merit and wisdom will be second only to those of the highest category. Those of the lowest category constitute *devas* and humans of all the worlds of the ten directions who aspire to rebirth in that land with sincere minds. Although they are unable to cultivate all the meritorious deeds, they should generate unsurpassed *bodhicitta*, concentrate exclusively on the Buddha Amitāyus up to ten thoughts (or moments), and vow to be reborn in his land with the utmost sincerity of mind. At the end of their lives, these people will dream of seeing that Buddha and will attain rebirth. Their merit and wisdom will be next to those of the middle category.

Section 2: Problems of Contemporary Humanity (*Xiandai renjian zhi kunao* 現代人間之苦惱)

The miseries and vexations of Jambudvīpa, our human domain, arise in three arenas: (1) problems of the external world, (2) personal problems, and (3) (383) social problems. Problems based in the external world include wind, rain, thunder, hail, frost, snow, drought, deluges, earthquakes, howling winds, eclipses, tsunamis, precipitous roads, snakes, tigers, and all such adversities. Personal problems include hunger, thirst, cold, heat, excessive desire, old age, being maimed and disabled, illness, premature death, and all such things that we suffer. Social problems include being burdened, being controlled, competition, being framed, imprisonment, being ordered about, conflict, being injured, love, separation, and all the resentments that come together to harm us.

Uttarakuru is far removed from the sufferings of the natural world and human society, but are not a few personal problems still present? Only in the Pure Land of Amitāyus is one completely removed from all suffering; that is why it is called Utmost Bliss. Currently, for human beings in Jambu[dvīpa] science has overcome nature and machines have extended human power, gradually alleviating the suffering that comes from the external world and within the self. However, there are still great disasters that science and machinery cannot overcome, such as typhoons, floods, earthquakes, tsunamis, diseases, pandemics, and so on. Instead, we frequently see them occur on a large scale, fouling the human realm and leaving no avenue for escape. We know the basic source of this to be the impure mental karma of sentient beings. If we depend solely upon material resources to put up resistance, in the end all we do is change form and move over to some other domain not of our choosing. In recent years Japan and other places have undergone great earthquakes that were horrible enough. However, forecasters in Australia predict that in three or four years, half the land masses and populations of Europe, Asia, and America could be lost (see the report in the *Shanghai News* for June 1926).

Alas! The human realm is a rotting house, the nation is in collapse, and there is no cover under which one may find safety. How terrible, how terrible! When we come to the misery of mass society, they multiply and get more severe by day and night and it is even more tragic! We teach the theory that human beings struggle for self-preservation like other living organisms, and from this (384) whatever we accumulate becomes a cause for killing and all that we do becomes an occasion for war and strife. Men and women, fathers and sons, elder and younger brothers, all fight and kill one another within the family; relatives, neighbors, fellow villagers, all fight and kill one another in the towns; gentry, farmers, laborers, and businessmen all fight and kill one another in society; and armies and politicians, legislators, and police all fight and kill one another in provinces and nations. With struggles in every territory, the opportunity brews for imperialist invaders "gone white" (*baihua* 白化) to come in to and commit slaughter on a mass scale; with all social classes pitted against one another, then the situation is ripe for mass slaughter by a dictatorship of the proletariat "gone red" (*chihua* 赤化). In this present generation, everyone is caught up and constrained in the factional fight between these two powers, the ones "gone white" and "gone red," and are rocked this way and that in fear and panic. No one can fathom it! Alas! Alack! Honestly, flames burn the sky in this world of poisonous smoke and the fires of war! Please! Take up our Buddhist slogan to "turn the Five Evils into the Five Virtues" so as to counsel everyone who has a mind to wake up!

A. The Buddhist Theories of the Five Evils, Five Kinds of Pain, Five Kinds of Burning, and Five Virtues (*Wu e, wu tong, wu shao, wu shan zhi foshuo* 五惡、五痛、五燒、五善之佛說)[8]

The Buddha said to Maitreya, "If in this world you are able to make your thoughts upright and your intentions correct, and if you refrain from the evils, this is considered the highest good! In the worlds of the ten directions, you will have no equal! Why is this? The *devas* and humans who dwell in all the buddha-lands practice virtue naturally and do not commit great evil, so they are easy to train. I became a buddha in this present world and dwell amidst the Five Evils, the Five Kinds of Pain, and the Five Kinds of Burning. This is the most severe kind of suffering. I teach and transform beings and cause them to abandon the Five Evils, be rid of the Five Kinds of Pain, leave the Five Kinds of Burning behind, subdue their wills, uphold the Five Virtues, reap good fortune and merit for themselves, and pass into the Way of long life and nirvana."

The Buddha said, "What are the Five Evils? What are the Five Kinds of Pain? What are the Five Kinds of Burning? What is it to extinguish the Five Evils and lay hold of the Five Virtues? (385) What is it to reap good fortune and merit and pass into the Way of long life and nirvana?

"The first evil is that of *devas*, humans, and all other creatures down to those that wriggle and crawl, who desire to commit every evil. There are no exceptions. The strong overcome the weak, and all turn and do harm to each other, injuring, slaughtering, and devouring one another. They do not think to cultivate virtue, and do evil and commit outrages until in the end they meet with disaster and punishment as they are naturally inclined. Deities keep records and offenders receive no leniency. This is why some are poor, lowly, beggars, lonely, deaf, blind, mute, stupid, wicked, handicapped, deranged, and unrestrained. [...] The world has a constant way: royal law sets up prisons, and those who do not fear them do evil, enter into crime, and receive their punishment. They seek liberation, but release is not easy to find. [...] In future rebirths after this life ends, it becomes

---

[8] This section consists entirely of a long quotation from the *Larger Sukhāvatī-vyūha sūtra* that runs from T12n0360_p0275c17 to T12n0360_p0277c25. However, Taixu skips over many passages, often breaking in the middle of sentences, and he inserts his own punctuation. I have retranslated the passage to reflect what readers of the original essay would have seen. I have indicated his omissions with ellipses ([...]).

ever more deep and severe. Entering into the gloom, they revolve in rebirth and receive [new] bodies, [...] and that is why there is the immeasurable suffering of the three evil realms. They change bodies, change forms, and change paths. Their lifespans may be long or short. [...] They are reborn alone, but meeting others whom they follow into a common rebirth, they go on retaliating against one another more and more, and the cycle never stops. Until their evil [karma] is exhausted, they cannot avoid each other. They revolve in this with no hope of escape, and liberation is difficult to achieve. The pain is indescribable! [...] These are the first great evil, the first kind of pain, and the first kind of burning, and the suffering they produce. It is like a great fire that physically burns people. If in the midst of this one can focus the mind, control thoughts, rectify conduct, and practice correctly, carrying out only the virtues and forsaking all evils, then one will reach emancipation and gain fortune and merit. They will pass beyond the world, surmount the heavens, and gain the way of nirvana. This is the first great good."

The Buddha said, "The second evil is that people of the world—fathers and sons, elder and younger brothers, family members, and husbands and wives—are all lacking in principle, disobey laws, are licentious and arrogant, and all do just as they please. They deceive one another, speak hypocritically, are false in word and thought, are sycophantic, and use clever speech to flatter others (386); they envy their superiors, slander the virtuous, and get embroiled in carping and calumny. Ignorant lords take on retainers who lack all restraint and seize all sorts of opportunities to trick them. [...] Ministers deceive their lords and sons deceive their fathers. Elder and younger brothers, husbands and wives, cousins and friends all deceive and cheat each other, every one harboring greed, anger, stupidity. Seeking their own advantage, they hanker after more things. The minds of superiors and subordinates above and below nurse this kind of mind. They squander their households and destroy themselves with no regard for what lies before or after. [...] The gods remember this and enter their names in a register, and when their lives come to an end and their spirits pass on, they fall into evil paths. Because of this, they naturally incur the immeasurable suffering of the three evil rebirths. They revolve around in these life after life for many *kalpas* with no means of escape. Liberation is difficult to achieve, and the pain is unspeakable! This constitutes the second evil, the second kind of pain, and the second kind of burning. It is like a great fire that burns people alive. If in the midst of this people can unify their minds and control their thoughts, assume the proper demeanor and rectify their conduct, practice all the virtues and avoid evil, then they will attain liberation and reap merit and good fortune. They will pass beyond the world, surmount the heavens, and gain the Way of nirvana. This is the second great good."

The Buddha said, "The third evil is that in this world the people live off one another while dwelling in the space between heaven and earth for a lifetime of uncertain duration. […] Those who are not virtuous constantly cleave to heresy and evil, and they think only on the pursuit of pleasure. They are wracked with vexation, thrown into confusion by attachment and desire, ill at ease whether sitting or standing, […] leer at voluptuous bodies, meet others illicitly, hate their own wives, sneak in and out, and squander the family's wealth doing what is unlawful. […] They indulge in whatever their hearts find pleasurable and exhaust their lives playing around. Or, while respecting the [rules of] seniority among their own relations, they may still transgress upon their dependents or others outside the family, boldly violating the king's laws and prohibitions. Such evil as this is apparent to both humans and devils and can be seen by the light of the sun and the moon. Gods take note of it and record it. Because of this, they naturally incur the immeasurable suffering of the three evil rebirths. They revolve around in these for life after life for many *kalpas* with no means of escape (387). Liberation is difficult to achieve, and the pain is unspeakable! This constitutes the third great evil, the third kind of pain, and the third kind of burning; such is their suffering. It is like a great fire burning people alive. If in the midst of this people can unify their minds and control their thoughts, assume the proper demeanor and rectify their conduct, practice only the virtues and avoid evil, then they will attain liberation and reap merit and good fortune. They will pass beyond the world, surmount the heavens, and gain the Way of nirvana. This is the third great good."

The Buddha said, "The fourth evil is that people of the world do not think of practicing virtue,[9] but lead each other to commit all manner of evil together: hypocritical speech, abusive speech, deluded talk, obscenity, flattery, theft, strife, and disorder. They undermine the wise and take delight in watching their ruin from the sidelines. They fail in their duties to their parents, are disrespectful to teachers and elders, do not keep faith with their friends, and are rarely honest. They hold themselves in high esteem and claim to have the Way. […] Having no fear of the gods of heaven and earth, sun and moon, […] they are constantly overbearing and arrogant. […] Gods and spirits remember all such evils. […] When their lives come to an end, all their evils will recoil upon them, and they will be naturally forced into a common destiny and captured. Also, the gods will keep a record, and they are drawn into calamity by their own faults […] with no means to escape trouble. They must march forward into the flaming cauldrons where their bodies and minds will be cut to shreds and they

---

[9] At this point in the text, Taixu inserts the phrases 轉上天、泥洹之道，是為三大善也。 I have skipped this in the translation and picked up where the sutra text continues according to the CBETA version of T.360.

will undergo mental anguish. Of what use will it be to repent then? Because of this, they naturally incur the immeasurable suffering of the three evil rebirths. They revolve around in these for life after life for many *kalpas* with no means of escape. Liberation is difficult to achieve, and the pain is unspeakable! This constitutes the fourth great evil, the fourth kind of suffering, and the fourth kind of burning; such is their suffering. It is like a great fire burning people alive. If in the midst of this people can unify their minds and control their thoughts, assume the proper demeanor and rectify their conduct, practice only the virtues and avoid evil, then they will attain liberation and reap merit and good fortune. They will pass beyond the world, surmount the heavens, and gain the way of nirvana. This is the fourth great good."

The Buddha said, "The fifth evil (388) is that the people of the world are irresolute and lazy, unwilling to practice virtue, discipline themselves, or ply a trade. Their families and dependents suffer hunger and cold, and when their fathers and mothers admonish them, they talk back with angry looks and do not follow their [parents'] directions. Instead, they disobey and go against them. They are like enemies, and having no sons at all would be better. […] They dawdle over wine and are addicted to beauty; they drink and eat to excess. They are heedless in their minds and loaf about; rash and domineering, they become vicious; having no understanding of human feelings, they force their desires on others. When they see people of virtue, they become envious and detest them. They lack righteousness, propriety, and self-reflection.[10] […] Their minds are constantly bent on evil, their mouths constantly speak evil, their bodies constantly carry out evil, and they have never had even a single virtue. They do not believe the sages of the past or the buddhas or the scriptures or the dharma. They do not believe that by practicing the Way they can liberate the world. They do not believe that after death they will take on a new birth. They do not believe that by doing good one reaps good and by doing evil one reaps evil. They want to kill *arhats* and sow dissension and confusion within the sangha.[11] They want to bring harm to parents, brothers, and dependents. All the six relations despise them and even wish to bring about their deaths. […] When their lives are about to end, contrition and terror arise in turn. They were unwilling to cultivate any virtue [previously], and just at the very end of life they repent, but what good comes after thus repenting? Between heaven and earth the five paths [of rebirth] are clearly distinguished; they are deep and dark, vast and boundless. The rewards of virtue and evil alternate between calamity and fortune that one bears by oneself; no one else can bear it for you.

---

[10] Taixu's text has 所顧難 here, while the sutra has 所顧錄. I have followed the sutra text.
[11] Here Taixu's text has 生眾, while the sutra has 眾僧. I have followed the sutra text.

Good people practice virtue, and for them pleasures follow upon pleasures, and they go from light to light. Wicked people practice evil, and for them suffering follows upon suffering and they go from gloom to gloom. Who can know this? Only the buddhas know. They teach and preach, but those who believe are few, samsara goes on without respite, and [beings fall into] evil rebirths without end. For worldly people such as these, it is difficult to give all the details. Because of this, they naturally incur the immeasurable suffering of the three evil rebirths. They revolve around in these for life after life for many *kalpas* with no means of escape. Liberation is difficult to achieve, and the pain is unspeakable! This constitutes the fifth great evil, the fifth kind of suffering, and the fifth kind of burning; such is their suffering. It is like a great fire burning people alive. If in the midst of this people can unify their minds and control (389) their thoughts, assume the proper demeanor and rectify their conduct, practice only the virtues and avoid evil, then they will attain liberation and reap merit and good fortune. They will pass beyond the world, surmount the heavens, and gain the Way of nirvana. This is the fifth great good."

The Buddha told Maitreya, "I say to you all: In this world the suffering brought about by the Five Evils is such that the Five Kinds of Pain and the Five Kinds of Burning arise and revolve in turn. [People] perform all manner of evil exclusively and they do not cultivate the roots of virtue, and so they all naturally fall into the evil paths of rebirth. It may happen that in this present life they are struck by an incurable illness. They want to die but cannot; they want to live but cannot. Everyone can see from this the retribution of evildoing. After death they accordingly enter into the three evil paths of rebirth where their suffering is immeasurable as they burn without any self-nature. This all comes from lusting after wealth and sex, and being unable to offer kindness to others, […] following their own thoughts and imaginings, they stupidly desire the things they chase after. They tangle themselves up in defilement and leave themselves no means of breaking free. To fatten themselves they quarrel with others over profit without self-reflection. Riches, honor, glory, prosperity: When rich they are pleased and feel no shame. They do not serve others or cultivate virtue. But their power does not last long and it runs out. They settle again in toil and suffering that gets worse over time! The way of heaven spreads everywhere, naturally bringing charges to the guilty. Its ropes and nets go both above and below, and feeling desolate and afraid, they get caught in them. It has always been this way. How wrenching is this pain!"

The Buddha said to Maitreya, "Such is the world. The buddhas take pity on it and use their supernatural powers to do away with evil and thoroughly inculcate virtue, to abandon [wrong] thoughts and uphold the sutras and precepts. Receive and practice the Way and the Dharma free from all faults, and in the end one will pass beyond the world and achieve the Way of nirvana."

The Buddha said, "All you *devas* and humans of present and future generations have received the Buddha's sermons and teachings. Can you familiarize yourselves with them and ponder upon them? If they can straighten their minds and behave properly, then at the summit the king will be virtuous and will lead those below them in [self-]transformation by circulating edicts which each will respectfully observe. They will revere (390) the sages and respect the virtuous, and they will espouse humanity, mercy, and universal love. Let the words of the Buddha teach and admonish them without daring to slacken their efforts. Seek to liberate the world and uproot the various evils of samsara. Leave behind the way of incalculable sorrow, suffering, and pain of rebirth in the three evil paths. Widely plant roots of goodness right here, spread kindness and consideration for others, and do not violate the prohibitions. Practice forbearance, diligence, single-mindedness, wisdom, and teach one another for the sake of goodness and to establish virtue. Rectify your minds and intentions, and keep the Eight Vows of Abstinence for a day and a night. This is superior to practicing virtue in the land of Amitāyus for a hundred years.

"Why is this? That buddha-land is effortless and spontaneous, and all [its inhabitants] pile up virtues without so much as a hairline of evil. Practicing virtue [in this world] for ten days and nights is better by far than practicing virtue in the buddha-lands in other directions for a thousand years. Why is this? In the buddha-lands of other directions there are many who practice virtue and few who commit evil. Good fortune and merit are natural, and there is no ground for creating evil [karma]. Only here [in this Sahā world] there is much evil and nothing comes naturally. [Beings] must strive in weariness to chase after their desires. They go around cheating each other with weary minds and worn-out bodies, drinking in bitterness and devouring venom. Carrying out evil in this way, they get no peace or rest.

"I pity all in the realms of *devas* and humans. I have gone to great pains to instruct you, teaching you to cultivate virtue, guiding you according to your capacities by bestowing the sutras and the dharma. None of you has failed to submit yourself. I have caused all of you to attain the Way as you wished. No state, city, or village to which the Buddha travels fails to receive his blessing. The whole land becomes peaceful and harmonious, sun and moon shine brightly, the wind and rain are timely, disasters do not occur, the state is prosperous and the people are at peace. Soldiers and weapons are of no use. [The people] revere virtue, revitalize their benevolence, and practice courtesy and yielding."

The Buddha said, "I pity all of you in the realms of *devas* and humans more deeply than parents think of their children. I became a buddha in this world to ameliorate the Five Evils, dispel the Five Kinds of Pain, extinguish the Five Kinds of Burning, counter evil with good, raise beings up from the bitterness of samsara, cause [beings] to attain the Five Virtues, and ascend to the peace of the unconditioned. After I have passed from this world, the sutras and dharma will decay and disappear. The people will resort to (391) flattery and deceit and take up the Five Evils once again. The Five Kinds of Burning will return as before the inception of the dharma, and they will become more severe as time goes on. I have not described it in detail! I only give you the gist of it."

The Buddha said to Maitreya, "You should all ponder this well! Teach and admonish one another just as in the buddhas' scriptures and dharma without incurring any infractions!"

At this, the bodhisattva Maitreya joined his palms and said, "What the Buddha has preached is profound and good! People of the world are such as this. The Tathāgata's mercy and pity reach to all, and bring all to liberation. I have received the Buddha's weighty instruction; I dare not violate or neglect it!"

B. Analysis of Viewpoints about the Human Realm (*Renjian zhi fenxi guan* 人間之分析觀)

Lao Dan [actually, Liezi 列子] said:

The Sage embraces similarity of understanding and pays no regard to similarity of form. The world in general is attracted by similarity of form, but remains indifferent to similarity of understanding. Those creatures that resemble them in shape they love and consort with; those that differ from them in shape they fear and keep at a distance. The creature that has a skeleton seven feet long, hands differently shaped from the feet, hair on its head, and an even set of teeth in its jaws, and walks erect, is called a man. But it does not follow that a man may not have the mind of a brute. Even though this be the case, other men will still recognize him as one of their own species in virtue of his outward form. Creatures which have wings on the back or horns on the head, serrated teeth or extensile talons, which fly overhead or run on all fours, are called birds and beasts. But it does not follow that a bird or a beast may not have the mind of a man. Yet, even if this be so, it is nevertheless assigned to another species because of the difference in form. Paoxi, Nü Gua, Shên Nong and Xia Hou had serpents' bodies, human faces, ox-heads and tigers' snouts. Thus, their forms were not human, yet their virtue was of the saintliest. Jie of the Xia dynasty, Zhou of the Yin, Huan of the Lu State, and Mu of the Chu State were in all external respects, as facial appearance and possession of the seven channels of sense, like unto other men; yet they had the minds of savage brutes. Howbeit, in seeking perfect understanding, men attend to the outward form alone, which will not bring them near to it.[12]

These are those who are human even though they do not look human, and those who are not human even though they have human form. These days, those who go in human form and are known as humanity [or the human realm, *renjian* 人間], but which are to be considered in the human realm, and which should not be so considered? In order to compare the superior and inferior among human beings and provide an analysis, please see the following chart (see pp. 88–91).

One may observe the human realm at present from the above chart. With the exception of an elite minority who keep their virtue pure or transcend both glory and dishonor, most have fallen into [rebirth as] barbarians—*asuras* or beasts—crawling animals, hungry ghosts, hell beings, not returning to the human realm. Is it not plain and manifest? Not only have they left the paths of human emperors and kings far behind, they are not even on the path of the tyrants!

Those who extend their strength to monopolize power to their own benefit and the detriment of others—these are the barbarians and *asuras*! Those who amass capital for their own enrichment, eating the substance of others to fatten themselves—these are the animals and beasts! Those who form the majority, whose capital is coerced, who labor without sufficient food or clothing—are they not the hungry ghosts? The multitudes who live under repression and pressure and cannot speak or act freely—are they not the denizens of hell? Contemplate this in silence; what kind of world is this human realm, and what manners of deeds are done in this human world? Can you not feel an outpouring of grief, and do tears of sorrow not fall? If one does not quickly realize one's errors in this and seek to improve oneself so as to return in time to the human path, then one is shameless in the extreme! For one who is bold and has a sense of shame, there is the construction of the Pure Land in the Human Realm.

Section 3: The Establishment of a Pure Land in the Human Realm (*Renjian jingtu zhi jianshe* 人間淨土之建設)

(395) Generally speaking, the construction of the Pure Land in the Human Realm arises from the various kinds of sadness, anxiety, and anger people feel

---

[12] This is the translation that appears in *Taoist Teachings from the Book of Lieh-Tzu* (see Giles 1912, 48–50). It appears that Taixu lifted this passage from Liu 2014 (1926), who inserted the phrase "Lao Dan said," which is not in the original text of the Liezi. I have adapted the Romanization for consistency.

超人間 Suprahuman				人間 Human	
佛 Buddhas	菩薩 Bodhisattvas	二乘聖者 Arhats of the Two Vehicles	天仙 Celestial Immortals	皇真人至人地仙 Thearchs, sages, realized persons, terrestrial immortals	帝聖人人仙 Emperors, saints, human immortals
				郅治,天降初民,北鬱單越 Governed benevolently, early descents from Heaven, Uttarakuru	大同,金銀銅轉,輪聖王 Great unity' gold, silver, copper wheel realms; Cakravartī-rāja
				化,無形 Transformative government, no punishments	教,象刑不用權力 Instruction, Symbolic punishment, no reliance on power
				無言 Without speaking	少言 Few words
				壽頗長 Long lifespans	壽命亦長 Also long lifespans
				鄰近超人 Near to superhuman	希在超人 Hope to be superhuman
				十善禪定 Ten Virtues and Samādhi	十善 Ten Virtues
				道 The Way	德 Virtue
	師 Masters	師 Masters	師 Masters	師 Masters	師君 Master ruler
				無為 Non-action	揖讓 Yielding
	無法 No dharmas	無心 No minds	無身 No bodies	人優游 Humanity at leisure	人有家 Humans with households
				尚樸 Simplicity abides	尚愛 Love abides

	人間墮落 Degenerate Human				
王君子賢人 Kings, princes, worthies	霸, 小人 Tyrants, inferior humans	夷狄修羅 Border tribes, asuras	傍生禽獸 Nearby birds and animals	餓鬼 Hungry ghosts	地獄 Hell beings
小康,鐵輪王,粟散王 Peaceful kingdom; Iron-Wheel king; Tributary kings	衰亂,王失福德 Decline and chaos; Unrighteous kings				
政刑,半用權力 Civil punishments, partial reliance on power	兵刑,用權詐 Martial law, deceit	專用權力 Reliance on power alone		大虎狼機,器為爪牙 Great banditry, weapons as claws and teeth	
號令 Orders issued	腕力 Coercion				
壽已短 Short lifespans	身陋壽短 Ugly forms, short lifespans	災禍恐慌 Disasters and desolation	朝不,保夕 Constant uncertainty and danger		
內聖外王 Sages or kings	假聖假王 False sages and pretend kings				
五戒 Five Lay Precepts	偽善 False virtue	十惡 五逆 Ten Evils and Five Heinous Deeds			
仁義 Humaneness and righteousness	假仁義 False humaneness and righteousness	假刑法名詞殺人 Killing under the pretense of justice			
君師 Enlightened ruler	大元帥 Military dictator	修羅虎狼羅剎惡鬼 Asuras, tigers and wolves, rākṣasas, evil spirits			
征誅 Punitive force	搜伐 Offensive attacks	優勝劣敗 Survival of the fittest			
人漸多 Humans gradually increase	人患多 Human anxiety grows	滅人國 End of human kingdoms	亡人種 Human extinction		
尚敬 Reverence abides	尚苟安 Respect and peace abide	尚戰爭 War and strife abide			

超人間 Suprahuman				人間 Human	
圓覺為性 Nature of perfect enlightenment	悲智空為性 Nature of compassion and wisdom of emptiness	但空為性 Nature only of emptiness	福愛樂變化為性 Nature of transient fortune, affection, and pleasure	淡泊自然為性 Nature of ease and sponteneity	樂生為性 Nature of pleasant life
				黃老 Huang-Lao	堯孔 Yao and Confucius
				忘公私 No distinction of public and private	天下為公 All is public/common
				老必出家 Elders must seek ordination	老必遜位 Elders must abdicate
				淡泊 Free and easy	火食 Cooking with fire
				春 Spring	夏 Summer
				解解超位 Universal contact, no status	精神上無一夫不獲 Superior spirit, not one person lacks
神游化身十方交通 Journey throughout the ten directions in transformation-body				諸星物質交通 Traverse all stars in material form	物質圓滿 Material fulfillment

			人間墮落 **Degenerate Human**
禮義節文為性 Nature of ritual, righteousness, and ceremony	誇詐成性 Nature of slander and deceit	恐怖成性 Nature of fear and horror	
禹荀 Yu and Xunzi	管商 Discipline and Shang [dynasty]	天演競爭 Evolutionary competition	
天下為家 All under Heaven as a family			殺人之父兄人亦殺其父兄 Killing the fathers and brothers of others and killing one's own father and brothers
不知出世 No knowledge of renunciation	爭權位 Struggle for power and position	爭權私利 Struggle for private advantage	
五味備 Preparing with the five flavors	縱漁獵 Fishing and hunting	極奢侈 Excess and luxury	
秋 Fall	冬 Winter	閏位 Imperial succession	
身體上無一夫不獲 Superior body, not one person lacks			
地球統一均田制產 Unified world, equal land distribution system			

超人間				人間				人間墮落			
佛	菩薩	二乘聖者	天仙	皇 真人至人地仙	帝 聖人仙	王 君子賢人	霸 小人	夷狄 修羅	傍生 禽獸	餓鬼	地獄
				郅治 天降初民 北鬱單越	大同 金銀銅鐵 輪聖王	小康 鐵輪 軍散王	衰亂 王失領德				
				化 無刑	教 象刑不用 權力	政刑 半用權力	兵刑 用權詐	專用權力	大虎狼猰 噐爲爪牙		
				無言	少言	號令	施力				
				壽頗長	壽命亦長	壽已短	身頗壽短	災禍恐怖	朝不 保夕		
				鄰近超人	希在超人	內聖外王	假聖假王				
				十善彌定	十善	五戒	僞善	十惡五逆			
				道	德	仁 義	假仁義	假刑法名詞殺人物			
師	師	師	師	師	師君	君師	大元帥	修羅虎狼刹恩鬼			
				無爲	異議	征誅	撻伐	優勝劣敗			
	無法	無心	無身	人優遊	人有家	人漸多	人患多	滅人國	亡人種		
				尙樸	尙愛	尙敬	尙苟安	尙戰爭			
圓覺 爲性	悲智空 爲性	但空 爲性	福愛變 化爲性	淡泊自 然爲性	樂生爲性	禮義節 文爲性	誇詐成性	恐	怖	成	性
				黃老	墨孔	禹荀	管商	天演競爭			
				忘公私	天下爲公	天下爲家		殺人之父兄人亦殺其父兄			
				老必出家	老必遜位	不知出世	爭權位	爭權私利			
				淡泊	火食	五味備	縱淫慾	恆奢侈			
				春	夏	秋	冬	閏位			
				辨辨超位	精神上無 一夫不獲	身體上無 一夫不獲					
神遊化身十方交通				諸星物質 交通	物質圓滿	地球統一 均田制產					

toward their present world. This gives rise to two types [of response]: First, they search for a pure realm outside the present world, such as rebirth in a heavenly land as taught in the theistic religions or in a Pure Land elsewhere as taught in Buddhism. Second, imagining how the present world could be made more ideal through local government, they hope to establish it by implementing reforms. The methods of improvement will differ according to the philosophical principles upon which they are based: they may be based upon materialism, idealism, biology, karmic dependent-arising, or based on dependent-arising in the storehouse consciousness. If the foundational principles are false, then the method will be riddled with errors and the search for ideal government based on them often devolves more and more into a destructive human environment. If on Marxism and materialism, it devolves into "going red" (*chihua* 赤化) characterized by class struggle as in the previous examples. In this section, I will discuss this under five subheadings:

A. What Is Needed to Establish a Pure Land in the Human Realm (*Jianshe renjian jingtu zhi yaoqiu* 建設人間淨土之要求)

1. The Buddha spoke of an era in which humanity would be born into the Heaven of Radiant Sound at the beginning [of a *kalpa*],[13] the human realm of Uttarakuru, the human realm under the rule of a wheel-turning monarch, and so on. These are some Buddhist ideas about establishing a Pure Land in the Human Realm.
2. Jesus' disciple St. Peter's communist[14] system, Saint-Simon's socialism, and Tolstoy's rustic lifestyle all are Christian requirements for establishing a Pure Land in the Human Realm.
3. The well-governed world of Laozi, Mount Weilei (畏壘, in the *Gengsang Chu* 庚桑楚 chapter), and the Land of Established Virtue (*Jiande zhi guo* 建德之國, in the *Shan Mu* 山木 chapter) of which Zhuangzi spoke, and

---

[13] Some Tiantai commentaries attribute the following to the *Madhyamāgama* (*Zhong ahan jing* 中阿含經): "As the *Madhyamāgama-sūtra* says in fascicle 12, those born in the world of the Radiant Sound Heaven during the beginning of the *kalpa* will hold men superior and women inferior. They will be born into this world together, and thus we say 'sentient beings' (眾共生世，故言眾生)." See *Miaofa lianhua jing wenju* 妙法蓮華經文句 by Zhiyi 智顗, T34n1718_p0055b19–b21. I am unable to find the corresponding text in the *Madhyamāgama*.

[14] As Justin Ritzinger notes, Marx's thought was not widely known in China at this time, so when Taixu uses the term "communism," he means something more like the anarcho-communist communes of his day. See Ritzinger (2017, 76, 98n1).

the lands of Huaxu,[15] Zhongbei,[16] Gumang,[17] and Damo[18] in the *Liezi* are all (396) Daoist requirements for establishing the Pure Land in the Human Realm.

4. Confucius' World of the Great Unity (*Datong* 大同), Mencius' well-field system, that which [Mencius] described as "King Tang with [only] seventy *li* and King Wen with one hundred *li*,"[19] while desiring to try [to rule] Teng with its fifty *li*[20] are the Confucian requirements for establishing a Pure Land in the Human Realm.

5. The ideal states of Socrates and Plato, the *Utopia* of Thomas More,[21] the *Nova Atlantis* of Francis Bacon,[22] Tommaso Campanella's *The City of the Sun*,[23] and James Harrington's *The Commonwealth of Oceana*[24] are all examples of ancient Western thinkers' desiderata for constructing a Pure Land in the Human Realm.

6. [Edward] Bellamy's [novel] *Looking Backward*,[25] [Theodor] Hertzka's *Freeland [: a Social Anticipation]*,[26] and [H. G.] Wells' [novel] *A Modern*

---

[15] In the "Yellow Emperor" chapter of the *Liezi* 列子, the Yellow Emperor visits the land of Huaxu 華胥 in a dream, the only means by which one may access it. He finds it a Daoist paradise in which the inhabitants act with perfect spontaneity. Upon awakening from his dream, he declares to his ministers that he has discovered the secret to ideal rulership. For an English version, see Graham (1990, 34–5).

[16] The country of Zhongbei 終北 appears in the "Questions of Tang" (*Tang Wen* 湯問) chapter of the *Liezi*. Aside from its ideal natural conditions, the feature that most likely appealed to Taixu was that its inhabitants lived without hierarchy of any sort; all were equals. See Graham (1990, 102–3).

[17] The country of Gumang 古莽 appears in the "King Mu of Zhou" (*Zhou Mu Wang* 周穆王) chapter of the *Liezi*. There the forces of *yin* and *yang* do not interact and the people sleep forty-nine out of every fifty days, and they believe dreams are real. See Graham (1990, 67).

[18] This reference is unclear.

[19] From *Mencius*, "Gong Sun Chou" 公孫丑上, a:3.

[20] *Mencius*, "Teng Wen Gong" 滕文公上, a:1.

[21] Thomas More (1478–1535) completed the *Utopia* in 1516 while in prison. In it, a visitor describes to More a place called Utopia in which there is no private property, everyone holds all things in common, and dines together in a great hall. See Baker-Smith (2014).

[22] Francis Bacon's *Nova Atlantis* depicted a society in which a commonly accepted revealed religion serves principally as a starting point for scientific inquiry. Science and religion work together to instill a discipline and attitude among people "which overcome[s] any craving for individuality." See Klein (2016).

[23] Tommaso Campanella (1568–1639) was a Dominican friar who wrote his *La Città del Sole* in 1602 while in prison for heresy and rebellion. In many respects, his description of the City of the Sun resembles the Buddhist mountaintop community Taixu will describe later in the Essay. Inhabitants of the City of the Sun hold all things in common and claim no ownership over spouses or children. See Ernst (2014).

[24] James Harrington (1611–1677) published *The Commonwealth of Oceana* in 1656. This book primarily advocates popular democracy and elected government. See "James Harrington (author)," at https://en.wikipedia.org/wiki/James_Harrington_(author), accessed November 4, 2017.

[25] Edward Bellamy (1850–1898) wrote *Looking Backward: 2000–1887* as a retrospective on the twentieth century from the point of view of Bostonians living in the year 2000. Its protagonist falls into a trance in 1887 and awakens in 2000 to a country transformed into a socialist utopia whose economy has been nationalized. Some scholars have suggested that Bellamy's vision owes much to the revivalism of the third Great Awakening in America. See Connor (2000).

[26] Theodor Hertzka envisioned a new utopian society to be established by occupying a stretch of uninhabited land in eastern Africa. The book was so popular that Freeland Societies took root in

*Utopia*²⁷ all exemplify modern thinkers and their desiderata for establishing a Pure Land in the Human Realm.

I have spoken about six types [of utopias] in summary form based only on what I can remember, but it is enough to get a glimpse of what desiderata for constructing the Pure Land in the Human Realm Eastern and Western people both past and present had in common. However, those who wish to create a Pure Land in the Human Realm in this way nowadays are all Buddhist, and their methods differ greatly from all the thinkers listed above. For this reason, we should first say a bit about the ingredients needed to constitute the Pure Land in the Human Realm.

B. The Ingredients for a Pure Land in the Human Realm (*Renjian jingtu zhi chengfen* 人間淨土之成分)

Systematic observation [shows that] all the Pure Lands of the ten directions throughout space have the Buddha, the Dharma, and the Sangha as their ingredients. Therefore, creating a Pure Land in the Human Realm will also require the Buddha, Dharma, and Sangha as ingredients. The one who is universally enlightened is called the Buddha. The Buddha manifests his body and land within the *dharmadhātu* and teaches the Dharma to sentient beings; this goes by the general name Dharma. The Sangha is that set of beings that dwell peacefully together and practice in accordance with the Dharma as taught by the Buddha. This is the concrete establishment of the actual Buddha, Dharma, and Sangha. (397) This should be the norm upon which we stand and the goal toward which we move. However, within our Human Realm, there are also the rationalized (*lixing* 理性) Buddha, Dharma, and Sangha.

Now we have quick, intelligent, and cognizing minds (*xinshi* 心識) that can be creative and can sustain us. This is the inchoate nature of the Buddha. Within, we have the body and its sense-faculties and the cognizing mind; without, there is the container world and the nation. The bodies and the karma of speech and conduct to which these internal and external factors give rise form the basis for the Dharma. The Buddha's enlightenment revolves around all the *dharmas*; the *dharmas* accumulate and manifest as the mind-Buddha (*xinfo* 心佛). They come together as the body, the household, the nation, the masses, as humanity (*renjian*

Austria and at least one expedition to the homeland of the Masai people in Kenya tried to make it a reality. See Bach (2011).

²⁷ Herbert George Wells (1866–1946) wrote *A Modern Utopia* in 1905 as part novel and part essay. The plot involves two men who, after a day of mountain climbing, find themselves inexplicably translated to a distant Earth-like planet where humans live in an ideal society. The book was hugely influential in the first quarter of the twentieth century. For a description and analysis, see Fokkema (2011, 290–4).

人間), and as the innumerable beings throughout the universe. This is the innate capacity (*benneng* 本能) for the Sangha.

In particular, we have been unable to understand thoroughly these three innate excellent Buddha-characteristics (*san dexiang* 三德相), which depend upon thoroughly realizing one's refuge in the Three Jewels. We manifest further lives, going from delusion to delusion, creating karma and experiencing its fruition. We crawl around in the Triple World, tossed on the waves into the Five Destinies, and arrive in this defiled Human Realm, unable to enjoy permanence, bliss, reality, and purity with the Buddha and the *āryans*. In the three [evil] destinies, we undergo pain; in the heavens we indulge in pleasure; only within the human destiny can we straighten out our minds and orient ourselves toward *bodhi*. Since we have gotten to the Buddha, Dharma, and Sangha as the basic ingredients of the Human Realm, we wish to lead people to grow them, helping turn this evil and turbid Human Realm into a virtuous and pure one. We must take refuge in the already-attained Buddha, Dharma, and Sangha as the predominating condition and foster them without backsliding. We must take the Buddha's prior enlightenment as our master, practice the same Dharma as the Buddha's ten virtuous deeds, and with the Sangha of the sages and worthies of the Three Vehicles as our companions build up the causes and conditions for a Pure Land in the Human Realm. For us to establish the Pure Land in the Human Realm, we must understand thoroughly the nature and virtues of the innate Buddha, Dharma, and Sangha and take refuge in the Buddha, Dharma, and Sangha as our basis.

C. The Way to Safeguard the Security of Life and Property (*Baochi shenming zichan zhi anquanfa* 保持身命資產之安全法)

(398) What the establishment of a Pure Land in the Human Realm requires is security of life and property. In brief, there are two ways to accomplish this.

(1) First, there are measures that get to the root, which we further distinguish into two:
   (1a): Attain rebirth in Uttarakuru, which one does by diligently avoiding the ten evil deeds of killing, stealing others' property, committing improper sexual acts, lying, double-talk, abusive speech, idle chatter, being greedy, being angry, and holding false views. So this depends upon each individual taking refuge in the Buddha, Dharma, and Sangha, and based on the power of the Three Jewels, making efforts

in the ten virtuous deeds and practicing the good karma that lifts the human condition. By reforming the individual mind, one builds the Pure Land in the Human Realm.

(1b:) One may strive in the practice of the Ten Virtues and pass on their spirit and teaching to transform the masses, expound virtue and ceremony to reform vulgar customs, work to end war and punishments, provide for the people's livelihood, help the young and give peace to the aged, recover waste, and bring comfort to the lonely. You could bring stability to the laboring and capitalist classes by ending corruption and bring peace between nations by getting rid of hatred. This is how one might create the Pure Land in the Human Realm by improving the human environment. Within this Pure Land in the Human Realm, security of life and property are maintained.

(2) Second, there are measures by which one may treat the symptoms [lit., "the surface"], of which there are also two types:

(2a) First, Buddhists from every country in the world could ask their several nations to give recognition and support to the organization of a large international association in accordance with the *buddha-dharma*. In times of peace they could cooperate in good works, encouraging and benefitting one another and refraining from causing each other trouble. In times of natural or man-made disasters where life and property are in crisis, this international Buddhist union could create the means to provide relief. One could consider which of the methods [outlined] in Layman [Zang's 藏] second letter to use.[28]

(2b) Based on all the Triple Gem's supernormal powers of "the inexhaustibility of the *dharmadhātu*" and "the nonduality of self and other," we should use the petitionary prayer methods of the Secret Mantra school to diminish calamities, augment good fortune, and quell the resentments of devils. We should also get the Buddhist union to practice repentance and prayers for fortune in times of need, so that we may turn misfortune into good fortune, and the

---

[28] As noted in the section "Other Influences" in Chapter 2, the two letters that Taixu's lay follower Zang Guanchan 藏貫禪 sent him provided a major impetus for the composition of this Essay. In both letters Zang proposed that Taixu take the initiative to found a global Buddhist organization in order to establish a "Pure Land in the world" (*shijie jingtu* 世界淨土). The second detailed more specific provisions about Zang's scheme than did the first.

inauspicious into the auspicious. This way, we could ensure the security of life and property.

If we could practice these methods for addressing both root and surface using both exoteric and esoteric means, then the causes and conditions would reinforce each other. If we can practice according to the Dharma, there would be no one who would be unable to maintain security.

D. Concrete Means for Establishing [the Pure Land in the Human Realm] (*Juti zhi jianshe* 具體之建設)

Although the Pure Land in the Human Realm encompasses all of humanity, it must still be realized in a concrete way if it is to manifest enough to make a material impression. The concrete establishment of this Pure Land in the Human Realm is close in Tibet and Thailand at present, but in China it would be best to establish it in the holy site of Mount Putuo. Otherwise, a deeply secluded, forested, marvelous place with fertile soil such as Great Wei Mountain might do, as long as it takes up the entire mountain and has a clear boundary.

Suppose we had a mountain with an area of ten square *li* that the country could give over for Buddhist use tax-free and that had plentiful springs of water, luxuriant bamboo forests, enough fields for rice and hemp cultivation to feed and clothe up to 20,000 people. We could build a great temple on a high plateau with a Shrine Hall dedicated to Śākyamuni Buddha as a general ritual space. We could add a lecture hall and monks' hall to the left as a residence for the Prajñā Assembly. To the right would be [another] lecture hall and monks' hall for the Lotus Sūtra Assembly. To the rear there would be a scripture repository. At the rear left there would be a Hall of Vairocana's Holy Huayan Assembly with a lecture hall and a monks' hall where the Huayan Assembly would reside. To the rear right there would be a Hall for the Vajradhātu and Garbhadhātu Maṇḍalas of Vairocana (400) along with an esoteric altar and monks' hall where the Esoteric Assembly would live. To the left rear there would be a Hall of Maitreya's Inner Court with a lecture hall and a monks' hall for the Consciousness-Only Assembly. To the right rear there would be a Shrine to the Blissful Land of Amitābha with a lecture hall and a monks' hall for the Pure Karma Assembly. At the left front there would be an ordination platform and a Vinaya Study Hall (*bantang* 板堂, a hall for advanced *vinaya* study) for the Precepts Assembly. To the right front there would be a Dharma Hall and a Meditation Hall for the Chan Assembly. According to this plan there would be 500 to 1,000 clerics and bodhisattvas. [Page 401 contains a diagram of these facilities.]

This would constitute the highest ocean of merit for the Pure Land in the Human Realm, and all of the Three Jewels would be fully present. The scripture repository would have books on Buddhism from all over the world in different languages (402) and be open to the public. The eight assemblies would all pursue the practices and studies of their individual schools. Only the Esoteric Assembly would practice daily rituals to avert calamities, increase fortune, and quell demons. Every day in the Buddha Hall the eight assemblies would gather to confess, pray for good fortune, and safeguard the Dharma to bring peace to the temple and the world.

On Śākyamuni Buddha's birthday there would be a joint meeting in the Buddha Hall to determine aims for the coming year. On his Enlightenment Day there would be a symposium[29] on doctrine to display each school's special accomplishment. Half a *li* in front of this would be a *śrāmaṇera* hall where the main business would be the reception of the *śrāmaṇera* precepts and training in each school's specialty for about 100 people. There would be two nuns' halls half a *li* to the right and left of this with *śrāmaṇerī* halls for about 400–800 nuns. These would emphasize the Vinaya and Pure Land schools. They would have set times for study with the assembly of monks. All of the above would constitute a compound just for monks and nuns, and would cover an area of four *li* square.

To the rear there would be a forested area of several square *li*, and beyond that would be an area reserved for devotees accommodating about 1,000 households of eight people each. These would be divided into three levels of villages for those who have undertaken the Ten Virtues, received the Five Lay Precepts, and taken the Three Refuges. Each level would consist of ten villages, and each village would accommodate thirty-odd households. The villages for those who have undertaken the Ten Virtues would lay closest to the clerical residences, and each household would receive 120 *mou* 畝 of arable land. The villages for those who have received the Five Lay Precepts would share a boundary with the villages for those who have undertaken the Ten Virtues, and each household would be allotted 100 *mou* of arable land. The Three Precepts villages would be next to the Five Precepts area, and each household would be allocated 78 *mou* of arable land.

Each village would have a village chief, and would manage two levels of primary school, have a preaching hall, a place for reading scriptures, and one

---

[29] I am provisionally using "symposium" to render *tongshu* 同樹 in the original text. I cannot find this as a term in any dictionary. The only sense I can make of it is that, since the Buddha's enlightenment took place beneath a tree, Taixu intends this to mean that the discussants would meet metaphorically under the same tree.

society for Pure Land practice. Each of the three levels would have a level-chief, the Five-Precepts villages would add a middle school, and the Ten Virtues villages would have both a middle school and a school for farming and forestry. The Three-Refuges level would house a police station with forty officers on patrol. The Five-Precepts level would provide four patrol captains, and the Ten Virtues level would provide one police chief who would have jurisdiction over the police who would patrol the entire mountain. The police chief would be selected by the Mountain President and would be under his command. Every year on the Buddha's Enlightenment Day (403), the Mountain President will cultivate practices for the alleviation of disaster at the shrine for the governments and people of all countries and all places.

The Mountain President will be elected by the nuns, *śrāmaṇeras*, people from the Ten-Virtues, Five-Precepts, and Three-Refuges levels who are at least twenty years old, and monks who have resided on the mountain for fifteen years since their ordinations and have traveled abroad for at least five years voting in primaries. Next, there is another election from among those elected during the primaries among the assembly of monks in the temple. He will have the authority to select the managers and representative board for the whole mountain.

They will establish a visitor's reception center in front of the land where the Three Refuges villages are to receive observers from all over. This will be staffed by one male and one female member of the clerical ranks, the Ten-Virtues, Five-Precepts, and Three-Refuges assemblies in order that all visitors may receive counsel.

Among the men and women on the mountain, marriage will be prohibited before the age of twenty, nor will they be allowed to seek ordination. Those that do seek ordination will maintain the state of *śrāmaṇera* for one to three years; [women] will maintain the status of *śrāmaṇerī* for two to five years; then they can enter the assembly of the fully ordained. They will live in the hall of one of the schools for four years—after this level they may not remain in the hall; next they will study in the halls of each of the schools for four years—after this level they may not remain further. Then they will dwell in a thatched hut or in a pagoda, take on a monastic office, or become a lecturer or a teacher, and so on. They will live in their thatched huts or pursue their responsibilities for five years—they may not extend this—and then they will travel abroad to convert [people] in every place beyond the mountain. Those who have been clerics on the mountain for fifteen years and then traveled abroad for five, or have lived on the mountain for twenty years will become chief clerics (*shouzuo* 首座) in the Eight Schools. These chief clerics will have the right to represent the Mountain President and consult in the affairs of the mountain. Each of the schools will pick two members, from among whom the Mountain President will select one for service in deciding all of the major matters.

This is the general plan for establishing a concrete Pure Land in the Human Realm.

E. Universal Ingathering (*Pubian zhi shehua* 普遍之攝化)

(404) One: This religious space will always be for government officials and citizens of all nations and places to practice for the amelioration of calamities, the increase of fortune, peace, serenity, and all people in the world will share in the benefit.

Two: When any nation or locality experiences a particular calamity, this religious establishment may entertain special requests from governmental or popular representatives from all countries and places for special prayer rituals for the prevention of calamities, the increase of fortune, peace, and serenity.

Three: Families and individuals from around the world may ask this religious establishment to practice special prayers for their own particular intentions.

Four: We will delegate bodhisattva-clerics with fifteen years or more of residency and practice to lead groups from the Ten Virtues, Five Precepts, and Three Refuges levels to travel around the world, transforming all people in order to bring about the Pure Land in the Human Realm.

Five: All governmental delegates, citizen's groups, and individuals are welcome to come here to participate and observe. We are eager to greet them and provide explanations of everything.

Six: At set times we will welcome Buddhists from every country and locality to come to the ritual spaces of all the schools of this mountain to study at their pleasure.

Seven: In order to unite the whole world, all Buddhists from this religious establishment and from around the world can make arrangements to proclaim the Dharma and convert all people.

Eight: We advise all the people of the world, for the protection of life and property and to plan for eternal life in Sukhāvatī, to contribute a portion of their wealth to this site to establish the Pure Land in the Human Realm. From this religious establishment will come timely rescue and eternal upliftment.

Section 4: The Pure Land in the Human Realm and Eternal Life and Utmost Bliss (*Renjian jingtu yu yongsheng jile* 人間淨土與永生極樂)

The Pure Land in the Human Realm safeguards life and property by means of the Three Refuges and the Ten Virtues, and puts the Three Refuges and Ten Virtues into practice by safeguarding life and property, but that is all. (405) One may extend one's life, but life still comes to an end and one dies. Since we believe that consciousness continues, takes on another body, and does not rest in oblivion, we thus must arrange for the "consciousness that continues to be embodied" a stable and appropriate basis in order to avoid the danger of going from delusion to delusion while bobbing up and down in samsara. However, having laid down the good roots of the Pure Land in the Human Realm based on the Three Refuges and the Ten Virtues, with the additional practice of invocation and transfer of merit, we gain ascent and rebirth in a pure land, either that of the Inner Court [of Maitreya] or of the [Land of] Utmost Bliss [of Amitābha] in the next life. One can examine the holy teachings for their testimony.

A. The Pure Land of Maitreya (*Mile jingtu* 彌勒淨土)

The Buddha said to Upāli: "Listen well! Listen well and reflect carefully! The Tathāgata, Worthy and Perfectly Omniscient, will now utter the prediction of the bodhisattva-*mahāsattva* Maitreya's future achievement of unsurpassed perfect enlightenment for this assembly. Twelve years from today his life will come to an end, and he will be reborn in the Tuṣita Heaven. At that time, the Tuṣita Heaven will be the abode of 500 myriads of millions of lesser gods (天子, *deva-putra* or *devatā*), every one of whom will practice the perfection of almsgiving. In order to make offerings to bodhisattvas who are one lifetime away from buddhahood, they use their divine powers to construct palaces [for them]. Each one of them sheds their sandalwood paste, *maṇi* gems, and jeweled crowns, kneels with palms joined, and utters this vow: 'This day I hold up these priceless gems and divine crowns in order to offer them before the assembly of *mahāsattvas*. May this person attain unsurpassed perfect awakening quickly in his next life, and may I thereupon receive a prediction [of buddhahood] in his magnificent buddha-land. May these jewels and crowns become the instruments of my success.' In this manner all the *deva-pūtras* will likewise kneel long and set forth noble vows.

"When all the *deva-pūtra*s have made their vows, their jeweled crowns (406) will all transform into 500 myriads of millions of jeweled palaces, each one having seven enclosing walls, each wall made of the seven jewels. Each jewel will emit 500 myriads of millions of beams of light, and each beam will have 500 myriads of millions of lotus flowers within it. Each lotus flower will transform into seven ranks of jeweled trees, each leaf of which will have the form of 500 myriads of millions of colored jewels, and each colored jewel will have the golden light of 500 myriads of millions of Jambu Rivers. From within each Jambu golden light will emerge a celestial maiden, each of whom will abide beneath the trees holding uncountable myriads of precious necklaces emitting wondrous music. At that time, declarations of the practices of the dharma-wheel of the ground of non-retrogression [will arise] from the midst of the music. These trees will produce crystal-colored fruit, and when beings enter into the midst of these fruits, then all the beams of light will rotate to the right and all sorts of sounds will issue forth to proclaim the *dharma* of great mercy and great compassion.

"Each one of the walls will be sixty-two *yojanas* in height and fourteen *yojanas* thick. 500 myriads of *nāga*-kings will surround these walls, and each of these *nāga*-kings will provide rain for the 500 myriads of rows of seven-jeweled trees that grace the tops of the walls. When a spontaneous breeze rustles these trees, they will brush against one another and proclaim the perfections of suffering, emptiness, impermanence, and no-self."

At that time, there was a great deity living in the palace named Lao-du-ba-ti (牢度跋提) who rose from his throne, offered obeisance to the buddhas of the ten directions, and put forth this noble vow: "If my merit makes me worthy to build a Hall of the Good *Dharma* for Maitreya, then may a pearl spontaneously emerge from my forehead." As soon as he made this vow, 500 myriads of gems spontaneously emerged from his forehead: lapis lazuli, mother-of-pearl, crystal, all of the colors were there in abundance such as azure *maṇi*-gems that shone both within and without. The light of these *maṇi*-gems wheeled throughout space, transforming into 49 kinds of fine and subtle jeweled palaces. Their balustrades were assembled from all of the *maṇi*-gems. Within these balustrades, nine hundred million *deva-pūtra*s (407) appeared by transformation, along with 500 myriads of *devī*s.

Uncountable myriads of seven-jeweled lotuses appeared in each *deva-pūtra*'s hand, upon each of which were uncountable myriads of lights. Within these light-beams were all sorts of musical instruments, and in this way celestial music sounded without their being played. As these sounds emerged, all of the *devī*s spontaneously took up a variety of musical instruments and accompanied the musical instruments with singing and dancing. Their songs proclaimed the Ten

Virtues and the Four Noble Vows. When the *devas* heard this, they all generated the unsurpassed Mind of the Way

At that time there were within the gardens rivulets of eight-colored lapis. Each rivulet had 500 myriads of jewels assembled together and all their waters had the eight excellent qualities. When the eight colors were all present, the water surged up among the bridges and trees.

Beyond the four gates, four flowers arose by transformation. Water flowed forth from these flowers like a gush of jeweled flowers. On each of the flowers there were 24 *devīs* with bodies of rare and subtle form as if adorned with the august bodily marks of a bodhisattva. In their hands 500 myriads of vessels spontaneously appeared. Each vessel was filled naturally with celestial elixir. On their left shoulders they bore innumerable jeweled garlands, while on their right shoulders they carried innumerable musical instruments. Like clouds in the sky they came forth from the waters praising the bodhisattva's six perfections.

If one attains rebirth in the Tuṣita Heaven, then *devīs* will spontaneously come in attendance. One will also have a seven-jeweled lion throne four *yojanas* high, and jewels as countless as the gold of the Jambu River will adorn it. Lotuses will sprout at the four corners and the head of the throne, each one made of a hundred jewels. Each jewel will emit hundreds of millions of light-beams both fine and wondrous that will transform into 500 million magnificent jeweled curtains of all gems and various flowers. Then *brahma*-kings from the ten directions by the hundreds and thousands will each bear a fine gem from the *brahma*-heavens as a jeweled bell to hang within the jeweled curtains, and then lesser *brahma*-kings will bring nets of jewels to hang upon the curtains.

At that time uncountable hundreds and thousands of *deva-pūtras* and *devīs* and their retinues will bring (408) jewels and flower to offer up to the throne. All of these lotuses will spontaneously bring forth 500 myriads of precious maidens holding white fly-whisks in their hands to stand in attendance within the curtains.

There will be four jeweled columns holding up the four corners of the palace, each of which will have hundreds and thousands of towers entwined by pure *maṇi*-pearls of Brahma. Then hundreds of thousands of *devīs* of incomparably wondrous form will appear among the towers holding musical instruments whose sounds will proclaim suffering, emptiness, impermanence, and no-self and all the perfections. In such a manner the celestial palace will have countless hundreds of millions of myriads of jeweled forms, and each of the *devīs* will have a jeweled form as well.

At that time, when the lives of the innumerable *devas* of the ten directions come to an end, they will all aspire to rebirth in the celestial palaces of the Tuṣita Heaven.

Then the celestial palaces of the Tuṣita Heaven will have five great deities: The first is called Ratnadhvaja (*Baozhuang* 寶幢) whose body rains down seven kinds of jewel that scatter within the walls of the palace, each of which transforms into a musical instrument. These will hang in the air and sound without being struck. They will produce innumerable sounds to suit the wishes of all sentient beings. The second is called Padmaśrī (*Huade* 華德). His body rains down a variety of flowers that cover over the walls of the palace and turn into a floral canopy. Each of these floral canopies ls led by a vanguard of hundreds and thousands of banners. The third great deity is called Gandharva (*Xiangyin* 香音). Every pore of his body rains forth a delicate ocean of sandalwood incense [billowing forth] like clouds. They create the colors of hundreds of jewels encircling the palace seven times. The fourth great deity is called Adhimukti (*Xile* 喜樂). His body rains forth wish-fulfilling pearls, each of which naturally fixes upon the banners and manifests and limitlessly proclaims refuge in the Buddha, refuge in the Dharma, refuge in the *bhikṣu-saṃgha*, as well as the Five Lay Precepts, the immeasurable good practices, all the Perfections, to benefit, advise, and assist in the intention of perfect wisdom. The fifth great deity is called Right Sound. Various kinds of water rain from all the pores of his body, and upon each kind of water float 500 myriads of flowers. Each flower has 25 jade maidens upon it, and all sorts of sounds emerge from the pores of their bodies superior to the music of any of the *devas* or demons.

The Buddha said to Upāli, "This is called the most excellent fortunate place that results from the Ten Virtuous Practices in the Tuṣita Heaven. If I were to abide in the world for a small *kalpa* and broadly expound the karmic rewards of the successor buddha (*buchu* 補處, i.e., Maitreya) and the fruits of the Ten Virtuous Practices for that entire lifetime, I could not exhaust them. For now, I will give an abbreviated explanation for your sakes."

The Buddha told Upāli: "If there be clerics along with all the great assembly who do not detest samsara and yearn for birth in a heavenly realm, longs for and reveres unsurpassed *bodhicitta*, and want to be a disciple of Maitreya, then they should perform the following contemplation.

"One who performs this contemplation should keep the Five Lay Precepts, the Eight Vows of Abstinence, the full precepts, be energetic in mind and body and not seek to cut off the afflictions, and cultivate the Ten Virtuous Deeds. With each and every thought they should reflect on the marvels and bliss of the Tuṣita Heaven. This is called correct contemplation; any other kind is called heterodox contemplation."

Then and there Upāli rose from his seat, adjusted his robes, made obeisance, and said to the Buddha, "O World-Honored One! The Tuṣita Heaven is possessed of such surpassing marvels and great bliss! When will this bodhisattva pass away from Jambudvīpa and be reborn in that celestial realm?" The Buddha said to Upāli, "First, Maitreya was reborn in Jieboli village (*Jieboli cun* 劫波利村)[30] in the land of Vārāṇasī, in the household of the great Brahmin Pravarī (*Bopoli* 波婆利). However, after twelve years, two months, and fifteen days, he returned to his original birthplace and assumed his seat in the lotus position as if to enter the meditative state of extinction (*mieding* 滅定). His body took on the color of purple gold, and he emitted a fiery red light as from a hundred or a thousand suns, and ascended to the Tuṣita Heaven. His remains appeared like an image cast in copper and gold and neither moved nor trembled. Within the nimbus of light surrounding his body the syllables "*śūraṃgama-samādhi*" and "*prajñā-pāramitā*" manifested brightly. Both humans and *devas* sought to erect a fine many-jeweled *stūpa* with which to make offerings to his remains.

"Then, within the Jeweled Palace upon the Seven-Jeweled Tower in the Tuṣita Heaven, he was instantly reborn by transformation, seated in the lotus position on a lion-throne. His body (410) was golden like the Jambu River with a height of sixteen *yojanas*, and he possessed in full the 32 major and 80 minor marks [of a great being]. The tufts of hair on top of his head were the color of lapis lazuli. His crown was adorned with a wish-fulfilling *maṇi*-gem and hundreds, thousands, tens of thousands, myriads of rubies. His celestial crown was of a hundred, ten thousand, myriads of colors, and within each and every color appeared countless hundreds and thousands of transformation-buddhas with transformation-bodhisattvas in attendance. Also in the crown were all the bodhisattvas from other places, exercising the eighteen supernormal powers as they wished with full self-mastery. There is a curl of white hair between Maitreya's eyes from which flows forth light of every kind with the colors of a hundred [kinds of] gem. Each and every one of the major marks has within it five hundred myriads of colors, as does each and every one of the minor marks. Each and every one of both the major and minor marks emits in profusion 84,000 clouds of light.

"He sits among all the *deva-pūtras* on their lotus thrones expounding the *dharma*-wheel of the practice of the stage of non-retrogression through the six periods of the night and day. Within each [of the six] periods, he brings 500 myriads of *deva-pūtras* to full accomplishment, establishing them in the non-retrogressive stage of unsurpassed perfect awakening. In that place within the Tuṣita Heaven, he expounds this Dharma night and day, liberating all the *deva-pūtras*. In 560 billion years according to time in Jambudvīpa, he will descend and take rebirth in Jambudvīpa, as the *Sūtra on the Descent of Maitreya* indicates."

---

[30] I have been unable to discover the original form of the name of this village.

The Buddha said to Upāli, "The name of this bodhisattva Maitreya while here in Jambudvīpa is the cause and condition for rebirth in the Tuṣita Heaven. After the Buddha's nirvana, if any of my disciples cultivates all meritorious practices with vigor, is of faultless deportment, sweeps [my] *stūpa* and spreads earth, makes offerings with varieties of renowned incense and fine flowers, practices the various forms of *samādhi*, enters into deep states of concentration, and reads and chants sutras, then someone like that should make his or her mind sincere. Even if one does not break the bonds of affliction, it will be as if one attained the six supernormal powers. One should fasten one's thoughts on contemplation of the Buddha's physical form and invoke the name of Maitreya. If people such as this for (or in) one moment take the Eight Vows of Abstinence, cultivate all kinds of pure karma, and (411) set forth great vows, then after their lives come to an end, they will attain rebirth seated in the lotus position on a lotus throne in the Tuṣita Heaven as [easily as] a great warrior extends his arm. Hundreds and thousands of *deva-putras* will perform celestial music, and they will scatter *mandārava* flowers and *mahāmandārava* flowers upon them. They will render praise, saying: 'Excellent! Excellent, O son of a good family! The lord of this celestial realm is called Maitreya. You should take refuge in him.' In response to their voices, [the ones reborn] offer worship. Having offered worship, they then contemplate the fine curl of white hair between Maitreya's brows in detail and pass beyond the guilt incurred in nine billion *kalpas* of samsara.

"At that time the bodhisattva (Maitreya) will preach the Dharma to them in accordance with their remaining past karma, establishing them firmly in the stage of non-retrogression and the unsurpassed mind of the Way. If beings such as this purify their karma entirely and practice the six ways of serving, then they surely and without doubt will achieve rebirth in the Tuṣita Heaven, encounter Maitreya, and follow Maitreya when he returns to birth in Jambudvīpa and be among the first to hear his Dharma. In the future they will encounter all of the buddhas of the good *kalpa* (*xianjie* 賢劫, Skt. *bhadra-kalpa*). In the constellation *kalpa* (*xingsu jie* 星宿劫, *nakṣatra-kalpa*) they will likewise encounter all the buddhas, world-honored ones. All of these buddhas will confer upon them predictions of their future awakening."

The Buddha said to Upāli, "After the Buddha enters nirvana, then if monks, nuns, laymen, laywomen, *deva-nāgas*, *yakṣas*, *gandharvas*, *asuras*, *garuḍas*, *kiṃnaras*, *mahoragas*, and all in the great assembly hear the name of the bodhisattva-*mahāsattva* Maitreya with joy and offer reverence and worship, then when their lives end, they will instantly attain rebirth [in the Tuṣita Heaven] as before with no difference. Those who only hear the name of Maitreya will not fall into dark places, border regions, heterodox views, and evil customs after they die.

They will always give rise to correct views, their followers will succeed [in their spiritual practices], and they will not slander the Three Jewels."

The Buddha said to Upāli, "[Even] if (412) sons and daughters of good families violate all the precepts and commit all manner of wrongdoing, hearing the great compassionate name of this bodhisattva, prostrating in obeisance, and confessing with a sincere heart will swiftly purify all of their evil karma. In future lives all the sentient beings that hear the great compassionate name of this bodhisattva; erect sacred images; offer incense, flowers, clothing, canopies, and banners; pay obeisance; and focus their thoughts will, when their lives come to an end, be welcomed by the bodhisattva Maitreya. The light from the curl of white hair between his brows will shine forth and all the *deva-putras* will scatter *māndārava* blossoms upon them. In an instant, these beings will attain rebirth [in the Tuṣita Heaven], see Maitreya directly, and bow their heads in reverence. Before they have even raised their heads again, they will hear the Dharma and be set in the unsurpassed stage of non-retrogression. They will encounter and pay homage to buddha-*tathāgatas* of the future as numerous as the grains of sand in the Ganges."

The Buddha said to Upāli, "Now listen well! This bodhisattva Maitreya will be a great refuge for sentient beings in the future. If any being takes refuge in the bodhisattva Maitreya, then you should know that that person will achieve the unsurpassed way of non-retrogression. Once the bodhisattva Maitreya becomes a *tathāgata*, *arhat*, and *samyak-saṃbuddha*, then these practitioners will see the buddha's light and receive predictions [of their own future buddhahood]."

The Buddha said to Upāli, "After the Buddha passes into extinction, then any among the four groups of disciples, *devas*, *nāgas*, demons, or spirits who wishes to attain rebirth in the Tuṣita Heaven should perform this contemplation: Focus your thoughts and reflect on the Tuṣita Heaven and uphold the Buddhist precepts. For one to seven days concentrate your thoughts on the Ten Virtuous Deeds and put them into practice. Dedicate the merit to rebirth in the presence of Maitreya. This is how you should contemplate. Performing this contemplation is like seeing a *deva* or seeing a lotus flower. If for one moment one can invoke the name of Maitreya, one can eliminate 1,200 *kalpas* of samsaric guilt. Just by hearing Maitreya's name with palms joined in reverence, one (413) will eliminate 50 *kalpas* of samsaric guilt. The one who worships Maitreya will eliminate a hundred, a thousand, myriads of *kalpas* of samsaric guilt. Supposing they are not born in the heavens, in the future they will still have a direct encounter [with the Buddha] under the Dragon-flower *bodhi* tree and give rise to the unsurpassed mind [of enlightenment]."[31]

---

[31] This long quotation is from the *Sutra on the Contemplation of the Bodhisattva Maitreya's Ascent to Rebirth in Tuṣita Heaven* (Foshuo guan Mile pusa shangsheng doushuaitian jing 佛說觀彌勒菩薩上生兜率天經), T14n0452_p0418c09–420c02.

B. The Pure Land of Amitābha (*Mituo jingtu* 彌陀淨土)

The Buddha then said to Elder Śāriputra: "A hundred thousand *koṭis* of buddha-lands west of here, there is a land called Utmost Bliss. There is a buddha in that land [named] Amitāyus who is preaching the Dharma at this moment.

"O Śāriputra, why is that land called Utmost Bliss? The beings in that land are free from all suffering and experience only pleasure. That is why the land is called Utmost Bliss. Again, Śāriputra, the Land of Utmost Bliss has seven rows of balustrades, seven layers of netting, and seven rows of trees, all of which are enveloped in four kinds of jewels. This is why it is called the Land of Utmost Bliss. Again, Śāriputra, in the Land of Utmost Bliss there are seven jeweled ponds filled with water having the eight virtues. Pure golden sands cover the beds of the ponds, and from the four sides of each pond rise stairs that combine gold, silver, lapis lazuli, and crystal. Above these stand pavilions also adorned with gold, silver, lapis lazuli, crystal, mother-of-pearl, red pearls, and cornelian. In these ponds are lotuses the size of cart-wheels, blue ones that give off a blue light, yellow ones a yellow light, red ones a red light, and white ones a white light. They are delicate, fragrant, and pure. Śāriputra, of such virtue and majesty is the Land of Utmost Bliss replete!

Again, Śāriputra, in that buddha-land celestial music plays continually, the ground is made of gold, and at the six periods of the day and night celestial *māndārava* flowers rain down. Every day, in the clear sunrise, the beings of that land take up cloth sacks filled with fine (414) flowers and go to make offerings to the hundred thousand *koṭis* of buddhas of the other directions and return to their own land in time to eat. They drink, eat, and then stroll about. Śāriputra, with such virtue and majesty is the Land of Utmost Bliss replete!

"Again, Śāriputra, there is always a variety of wonderful birds of every color: white cranes, peacocks, parrots, mynahs, *kalaviṅka*, and *jīvajīva* birds. During the six periods of the day and night they sing with harmonious and elegant voices, and the sound proclaims the Five Roots, the Five Powers, the Seven Factors of Enlightenment, the Noble Eightfold Path, and other such teachings. Whenever the beings of the land hear these sounds, their thoughts fix upon the Buddha, the Dharma, and the Sangha. O Śāriputra, do not say that these birds were born as the result of evil karma! Why is that? Because that buddha-land lacks the three evil destinies. O Śāriputra, even the names of the three evil destinies do not occur in that buddha-land; how much less would their reality. Amitāyus manifests all of these birds by transformation out of his wish to cause the sound of the Dharma to flow and spread widely.

"O Śāriputra! When gentle breezes blow in that buddha-land, rustling the ranks of jeweled trees and netting, marvelous sounds come forth as if a hundred thousand different musical instruments had started to play all together. Those that hear the sounds spontaneously give rise to a mind reflecting upon the Buddha, the Dharma, and the Sangha. Śāriputra, with such virtue and majesty is that buddha-land replete!

"O Śāriputra! What do you think? Why is that Buddha named 'Amita'?[32] Śāriputra, that Buddha's light is immeasurable and illuminates all the lands in the ten directions without hindrance. This is why he is called Amitābha. Also, Śāriputra, the lifespans of that Buddha and all the inhabitants [of his buddha-land] are immeasurable, spanning limitless incalculable *kalpas*. This is why he is called Amitāyus. Śāriputra, It has been ten *kalpas* since Amitābha attained buddhahood. Moreover, Śāriputra, that Buddha has innumerable, unbounded *śrāvaka* disciples, every one an *arhat*. One cannot (415) reckon their number. The same is true of his assembly of bodhisattvas. Śāriputra, with such virtue and majesty is that buddha-land replete!

"Again, Śāriputra, all sentient beings born in the Land of Utmost Bliss abide in the stage of non-retrogression. Many of them will become buddhas after one more life. Their number is so great that it is beyond reckoning; one can only say that they are innumerable, unlimited, and incalculable.

"O Śāriputra, sentient beings who hear this should generate an aspiration, a vow to attain birth in that land. What is the reason? It will enable them to gather in one place with all the sages of superior virtue. Śāriputra, one cannot attain rebirth in that land based only on a few roots of goodness or a small store of fortune and virtue. Śāriputra, if sons or daughters of good families hear of Amitāyus Buddha and hold his name for one day, two days, three days, four days, five, six, or seven days with a single, unperturbed mind, then at the end of their lives, Amitābha will manifest before them with all of his holy retinue. Those persons' minds will not be upended at the last moment, and they will instantly attain rebirth in Amitāyus's Land of Utmost Bliss.

"O Śāriputra! I have seen these benefits, and thus I declare: Anyone who hears this preaching should aspire to attain rebirth in that land."[33]

---

[32] I have translated *Amituo* 阿彌陀 here simply as "Amita" because the Chinese characters only represent those three syllables, and the text will expound on both versions of this Buddha's name, "Amitābha" and "Amitāyus." Because of this, it seemed inappropriate to use one or the other of these forms here.

[33] This quotation comes from the *Shorter Sukhāvatī-vyūha-sūtra* 佛說阿彌陀經, at T.366, p. 12: 346c10–347b8.

C. The Pure Land of the Ocean of Awakening
(*Juehai jingtu* 覺海淨土)

Even though we spoke before about the features that distinguish the Impure Lands of the Five Destinies, the Pure Land in the Human Realm, the Pure Land of [Maitreya's] Inner Court, and the Pure Land of Utmost Bliss, one must understand that each and every identifying feature is beyond words and thoughts, and so all are equally subsumed under the *Tathatā-dharmatā* Pure Land. In particular, without the bodhisattva's non-discriminating wisdom, one cannot have a partial realization of purity; without the Tathāgata's wisdom of the great, perfect Ocean of Awakening (416), one cannot have a complete realization of purity. Therefore, all manner of distinctions appear. Even with all these apparent distinctions, no one is apart from the Ocean of Awakening.

However, from the specific [mix of] defilement and purity in the mind of awakening, in which the defilements can be light or heavy and purity can be partial or perfected, all distinctions manifest. Because of the defilements in the beginningless mind of awakening, afflicted karma (*huoye* 惑業) accumulates and taints the mind of awakening. These defilements in the mind of awakening [in turn] increase afflicted actions, leading the tainted mind of awakening to manifest as the Impure Land of the Five Destinies. By decreasing and quelling the deluded karma and increasing virtuous karma, one calls virtue into the mind of awakening, which then manifests as the Pure Land in the Human Realm.

Relying on the pure vows of Maitreya and Amitābha as contributory conditions, one quells the afflicted actions and increases pure actions leading to the purification of the mind of awakening, which then manifests as the pure land of the Inner Court [of Maitreya in the Tuṣita Heaven] or the Pure Land of Utmost Bliss [of Amitābha]. Within the great ocean of the mind of awakening there is a small part not yet purified, because of which one cannot thoroughly differentiate all characteristics. The Tathāgata's Ocean of Awakening is perfectly pure, and the marks of suchness comport with the suchness of the *dharma*-nature; this is called the *saṃbhoga* Pure Land (or Pure Land for the Buddha's Enjoyment; *zi shouyong zhi jingtu* 自受用之淨土). However, in order that bodhisattvas at all stages of progress may enjoy it together, along with those of the Three Vehicles and the Five Destinies, he also manifests all pure and impure bodies and lands as if by magical transformation with inexhaustible distinctions. Know that in the Ocean of Awakening, they are all together in the Pure Land! If one wishes to plumb the meaning of this, it is all contained in the teaching, principle, practices, and fruition of the Mahayana Dharma.

Section 5: Taking One's Own Vows of Compassion and Charitable Deeds as the Starting Point (*You benren fa da beiyuan shihe wei shi* 由本人發大悲願施捨為始)

We have realized how to establish the Pure Land in the Human Realm. If we wish to establish this Pure Land in the Human Realm, we must begin by looking deeply to ourselves. Right now, this human realm is undergoing various kinds of conflict and disaster, various acts of deceit, plunder, licentiousness, and drunkenness. Natural and man-made calamities cause the Five Kinds of Burning and the Five Kinds of Pain to pour in on us without letup. It is bitter beyond words! Out of the arising of great pity, with mind and body wracked by pain, make great vows to bring about the Pure Land in the Human Realm as a means of rescue. One must be aware that the completion of a pure land has never (417) arisen as a result of anything except the fulfillment of compassionate vows. Amitābha's realized land arose from the fulfillment of the compassionate vows that the bodhisattva Dharmākara made while still at the causal stage. As it is said in the *Longer Sukhāvatī-vyūha-sūtra*:

1. The first vow: "If, when I attain buddhahood, the paths of the hells, hungry ghosts, or animals form any part of my land, then I will not accept full awakening."
2. The second vow: "If, when I attain buddhahood, the *devas* and humans of my land re-enter the three evil paths after they pass away, then I will not accept full awakening."
3. The third vow: "If, when I attain buddhahood, the *devas* and humans of my land are not wholly the color of true gold, then I will not accept full awakening."
4. The fourth vow: "If, when I attain buddhahood, the *devas* and humans of my land are not uniformly comely, then I will not accept full awakening."
5. The fifth vow: "If, when I attain buddhahood, the *devas* and humans of my land should not be aware of their deeds in previous lives going back at least a hundred thousand *koṭis* of *nayutas* of *kalpas*, then I will not accept full awakening."
6. The sixth vow: "If, when I attain buddhahood, the *devas* and humans of my land do not attain the divine eye enabling them to see buddha-lands at least to the number of a hundred thousand *koṭis* of *nayutas*, then I will not accept full awakening."

7. The seventh vow: "If, when I attain buddhahood, the *devas* and humans of my land do not attain the divine ear enabling them to see and hear [*sic*] the preaching of at least a hundred thousand *koṭis* of *nayutas* of buddhas and if they do not accept and uphold all of it, then I will not accept full awakening."
8. The eighth vow: "If, when I attain buddhahood, the *devas* and humans of my land do not attain the cognition of others' minds, enabling them to know the thoughts of all the beings in at least a hundred thousand *koṭis* of *nayutas* of buddha-lands, then I will not accept full awakening."
9. The ninth vow: "If, when I attain buddhahood, the *devas* and humans of my land do not attain the power to travel beyond at least a hundred thousand *koṭis* of *nayutas* of buddha-lands in an instant, then I will not accept full awakening."
10. The tenth vow: "If, when I attain buddhahood, the *devas* and humans of my land give rise to self-attachment, then I will not accept (418) full awakening."
11. The eleventh vow: "If, when I attain buddhahood, the *devas* and humans of my land do not abide in the class of beings who are definitely bound for liberation, then I will not accept full awakening."
12. The twelfth vow: "If, when I attain buddhahood, my light has any limitation and does not illuminate at least a hundred thousand *koṭis* of *nayutas* of buddha-lands, then I will not accept full awakening."
13. The thirteenth vow: "If, when I attain buddhahood, my lifespan has any limitation and does not extend to at least a hundred thousand *koṭis* of *nayutas* of *kalpas*, then I will not accept full awakening."
14. The fourteenth vow: "If, when I attain buddhahood, the number of *śrāvakas* in my land can be reckoned even by the beings all becoming *pratyekabuddhas* in the great trichiliocosm counting all together for a hundred thousand *kalpas*, then I will not accept full awakening."
15. The fifteenth vow: "When I attain buddhahood, the lifespan of the *devas* and humans in my land will be limitless,[34] with the exception of those who have made fundamental vows to shorten their cultivation of their own free will. If any of this is not so, then I will not accept full awakening."

---

[34] Taixu's citation has *neng wuxian liang* 能無限量, "can be limitless," while the Taishō and previous versions has *wuneng xianliang* 無能限量, "will not be limitable." The difference is slight and does not seem to affect the meaning.

16. The sixteenth vow: "If, when I attain buddhahood, the *devas* and humans in my land so much as hear of anything that is not virtuous, then I will not accept full awakening."
17. The seventeenth vow: "If, when I attain buddhahood, all the innumerable buddhas of the ten directions do not exalt my name, then I will not accept full awakening."
18. The eighteenth vow: "When I attain buddhahood, if all the sentient beings of the ten directions who wholeheartedly rejoice and have faith and wish to be born in my land even for only ten thoughts do not achieve birth, then I will not accept full awakening. I exclude only those who have committed the Five Heinous Deeds or slandered the correct dharma."
19. The nineteenth vow: "When I attain buddhahood, if I and my entire retinue do not appear all around any sentient being of the ten directions who has generated the mind of enlightenment, cultivated all forms of merit, and wholeheartedly generated the vow to be born in my land at their life's end, then I will not accept full awakening."
20. The twentieth vow: "When I attain buddhahood, if any of the sentient beings of the ten directions who have heard of my name, focused their thoughts on my land, planted roots of virtue, and wholeheartedly dedicated the merit to their desire for birth in my land fail to obtain their goal, then I will not accept full awakening." (419)
21. The twenty-first vow: "If, when I attain buddhahood, any of the *devas* and humans in my land does not have the 32 bodily marks of a great being in full, then I will not accept full awakening."
22. The twenty-second vow: "When I attain buddhahood, all the bodhisattvas of other buddha-lands will attain rebirth in my land in the stage of those who will attain buddhahood in their next life. I exclude those who take fundamental vows to teach for the sake of sentient beings. Covered by the armor of their great vows and accumulating roots of virtue, they will liberate one and all. Traveling to all the buddha-lands, cultivating bodhisattva practices, making offerings to all the buddhas-*tathāgatas* of the ten directions, giving guidance to sentient beings as numberless as the sands of the Ganges, they will establish them in the unsurpassed true path. Going beyond the ordinary practices of the [ten] stages, they will present the practices of Samantabhadra before others. If this does not come to pass, then I will not accept full awakening."
23. The twenty-third vow: "If, when I attain buddhahood, the bodhisattvas in my land cannot avail themselves of a buddha's supernormal power in order

to make offerings to all buddhas, traveling to innumerable *koṭis* of *nayutas* of other buddha-lands in the space of a single meal-time, then I will not accept full awakening."

24. The twenty-fourth vow: "If, when I attain buddhahood, the bodhisattvas in my land cannot display their roots of virtue and produce whatever offerings they wish to make before all buddhas, then I will not accept full awakening."

25. The twenty-fifth vow: "If, when I attain buddhahood, the bodhisattvas in my land cannot preach all-encompassing wisdom, then I will not accept full awakening."

26. The twenty-sixth vow: "If, when I attain buddhahood, the bodhisattvas in my land do not attain a body like that of Vajra-Nārāyaṇa, then I will not accept full awakening."

27. The twenty-seventh vow: "When I attain buddhahood, the *devas* and humans in my land as well as all the myriads of things in it will be glorious and pure, luminous and lovely. Their forms will be completely unique, exquisitely subtle, exceedingly wonderful, and beyond measure. If beings, even those who have attained the divine eye, will not be able [sic] to fathom and distinguish their names and number, then I will not accept full awakening."[35]

28. The twenty-eighth vow: "If, when I attain buddhahood, the bodhisattvas in my land, down to the ones with the least merit, are unable to see (420) its *bodhi*-tree with its form of immeasurable light and height of four million *li*, then I will not accept full awakening."

29. The twenty-ninth vow: "If, when I attain buddhahood, the bodhisattvas in my land receive and study the teachings of the sutras, chant them, uphold them, and preach them, but without developing eloquence and discernment, then I will not accept full awakening."

30. The thirtieth vow: "If, when I attain buddhahood, there are any limits to the wisdom and eloquence of the bodhisattvas in my land, then I will not accept full awakening."

31. The thirty-first vow: "When I attain buddhahood, [my land will be pure; its light will illuminate and][36] make visible immeasurable, innumerable,

---

[35] The text has 不能明了辨其名數者, which I have translated "will not be able [sic] to understand and distinguish their names and number," which makes little sense. However, the Taishō version has 有能明了辨其名數者, or "are able to understand, etc.," which makes sense. See T12n0360_p0268b25–b28.

[36] The edition from which I made this translation lacked this phrase from the sutra.

inconceivable buddha-worlds as if seeing one's own face in a clear mirror. If this is not so, then I will not accept full awakening."

32. The thirty-second vow: "When I attain buddhahood, all the palaces, towers, ponds and streams, flowers and trees, the land, and absolutely everything from the ground up to the sky, will all be knit together from countless jewels and a hundred thousand kinds of incense. All will be marvelously arrayed, surpassing [the abodes of] *devas* and humans. Its incense will pervade the worlds of the ten directions, and all the bodhisattvas who hear of it will engage in buddha-practices. If it is not thus, then I will not accept full awakening."

33. The thirty-third vow: "When I attain buddhahood, the various classes of beings dwelling in countless inconceivable buddha-worlds in all the ten directions who are touched by my light will find their bodies and minds becoming more soft and supple than *devas* and humans. If it is not so, then I will not accept full awakening."

34. The thirty-fourth vow: "If, when I attain buddhahood, the various classes of beings dwelling in countless inconceivable buddha-worlds in all the ten directions do not attain the bodhisattva's forbearance of the unborn and the various profound *dhāraṇīs*, then I will not accept full awakening."

35. The thirty-fifth vow: "If, when I attain buddhahood, the women dwelling in countless inconceivable buddha-worlds in all the ten directions who hear of my name rejoice and in joyful faith generate the mind of enlightenment, despise their female bodies, and yet at the end of their lives are reborn again in female form, then I will not accept full awakening."

36. The thirty-sixth vow: "When I attain buddhahood, (421) the bodhisattvas of countless inconceivable buddha-worlds in all the ten directions will hear of my name, and after they pass away will continually cultivate *brahma-*conduct in subsequent lives until they complete the buddha-way. If it is not so, then I will not accept full awakening."

37. The thirty-seventh vow: "When I attain buddhahood, the divine and human inhabitants of countless inconceivable buddha-worlds in all the ten directions will hear of my name, prostrate themselves and bow their heads in worship. In joy and faith they will pursue bodhisattva practices. No one among the *devas* and humans of the world will fail to revere them. If it is not so, then I will not accept full awakening."

38. The thirty-eighth vow: "If, when I attain buddhahood, the *devas* and humans of my land desire clothing, and the splendid robe praised by the buddhas does not instantly and spontaneously materialize upon their

bodies, or if these robes should ever need stitching, dyeing, or washing, then I will not accept full awakening."
39. The thirty-ninth vow: "If, when I attain buddhahood, the joy that the *devas* and humans of my land receive does not match that of an *arhat*, then I will not accept full awakening."
40. The fortieth vow: "If, when I attain buddhahood, the bodhisattvas in my land who wish to view immeasurable buddha-lands in all the ten directions should not see them right then illuminated in the jeweled trees as one sees one's face in a clear mirror, then I will not accept full awakening."
41. The forty-first vow: "If, when I attain buddhahood, any of the bodhisattvas of other lands who hear my name, even those on the verge of attaining buddhahood, have defective or incomplete sense faculties, then I will not accept full awakening."
42. The forty-second vow: "When I attain buddhahood, the bodhisattvas of other lands who hear my name will attain the *Samādhi* of Purity and Liberation. While still in this *samādhi*, they will be able to present offerings to the buddhas in immeasurable, inconceivable buddha-lands in an instant without breaking their concentration. If it is not so, then I will not accept full awakening."
43. The forty-third vow: "When I attain buddhahood, the bodhisattvas of other lands who hear my name (422) will all be reborn into noble families in subsequent lives. If it is not so, then I will not accept full awakening."
44. The forty-fourth vow: "When I attain buddhahood, the bodhisattvas of other lands who hear my name will leap for joy, cultivate bodhisattva practices, and bring their roots of virtue to completion. If it is not so, then I will not accept full awakening."
45. The forty-fifth vow: "When I attain buddhahood, the bodhisattvas of other lands who hear my name will all attain the *Samādhi* of Universal Equality. From their attainment of this *samādhi* to the time they achieve buddhahood, they will be able to view all the immeasurable, inconceivable, buddhas continually. If it is not so, then I will not accept full awakening."
46. The forty-sixth vow: "When I attain buddhahood, the bodhisattvas in my land will be able to hear spontaneously whatever *dharma* they wish. If it is not so, then I will not accept full awakening."
47. The forty-seventh vow: "If, when I attain buddhahood, the bodhisattvas in other lands do not instantly attain the stage of non-retrogression upon hearing my name, then I will not accept full awakening."

48. The forty-eighth vow: "If, when I attain buddhahood, the bodhisattvas in other lands do not instantly attain the first, second [and third] [*dharma-*] endurance, or the stages of non-retrogression of all buddha-*dharmas*, then I will not accept full awakening."[37]

Looking at the first vow, that is, that his Pure Land would be devoid of the suffering of the three evil destinies, the fact that in vow after vow after vow [the land] would be devoid of all obstacles and troubles, and the fact that his vows gather in all suffering sentient beings for rebirth [there], one can know that these vows arose from his great pity for suffering beings. In the end, the vows were fulfilled and now there is the [Land of] Utmost Bliss. However, had he not begun his religious practice with offerings, he would not have been able to set forth these genuine great vows. If he had not made offerings because of clinging to his present short life and meager property, he would not have been able to pursue sincerely the greater and more expansive (423) *dharma*-body and *dharma*-property. If he had not given up his present fragile body and property because of greed, he would not have been able to transform them into the body and property of the [Land of] Utmost Bliss. Thus, he had to begin by giving up his kingship and country to become the bodhisattva Dharmākara. He was able to give up his country, so there was no worldly treasure he could not give up; He was able to relinquish his kingship, so there was nothing about his enjoyment-body that he could not offer up. In China of old there were many who offered up their houses and fortunes as Buddhist monasteries; they gave up their own bodies or their children and grandchildren into the service of the Three Jewels. If today you wish to put the vows to establish the Pure Land in the Human Realm into practice, begin there and afterwards it will be possible. Otherwise, the vows will be vain and will produce results only with difficulty. From generating the mind to make offerings such as this for all humanity, to causing all of humanity to escape suffering and attain bliss, to serving the Three Jewels and the people of the world, the myriad good practices will all be fulfilled. Practice with firmness and seek not to backslide. This is why the *Longer Sukhāvatī-vyūha-sūtra* says:

After setting forth his vows, Dharmākara spent

inconceivable *kalpas* amassing immeasurable roots of moral conduct for himself. No consciousness of desire, no consciousness of anger, and no consciousness of harmful intent arose in him, nor did any thoughts of desire, anger, or harmful

---

[37] The quotation is from T12n0360_p0267c17–269b06, though Taixu did not use the current Taishō version.

intent. He did not grasp at the *dharmas* of form, sound, smell, taste, or touch. His endurance reached perfection, he gave no thought to [his own] suffering, he minimized his desires and came to know contentment, and he was untainted by hatred and delusion. He was constantly immersed in the tranquility of *samādhi*, his wisdom was unobstructed, and his mind contained no hypocrisy or deceit. He maintained a pleasing countenance and used loving words, and could anticipate others' thoughts in answering their questions. He strode forward heroically, and his aspiration never gave out. He sought only the clear, pure Dharma in order to benefit all the masses of beings by his wisdom. He paid reverence to the Three Jewels and served his teachers and elders in order to perform all his practices with great dignity and bring the merit of all sentient beings to completion.

He abided in the *dharmas* of emptiness, signlessness, and wishlessness, and he contemplated phenomena as uncreated and unarisen, like magical transformations. He distanced himself from coarse talk and brought no harm to himself, to others, or to both self and others. He practiced virtuous speech, the kind that brought benefit to himself, to the people (424), or to both himself and the people together. He gave up his country and relinquished his kingship, and abjured both wealth and body. He practiced the Six Perfections himself, and taught others to do so. For countless *kalpas* he accumulated virtues and piled up merit.

Wherever he was born, immeasurable treasure spontaneously appeared just as he wished. He taught, converted, and established countless sentient beings on the unsurpassed, true, and correct path. He might [be reborn as] an elder householder, a lay devotee, a highborn aristocrat, a warrior-king, or a great world-sovereign. He might appear as a *deva*-king in one of the six desire heavens or [any kind of *deva*] up to Brahmā. He constantly presented the four kinds of offering to pay reverence to all the buddhas. The merit of all this cannot be put into words. His breath was fragrant and clean like a lotus flower, and the fragrance of sandalwood came forth from every pore of his body, universally pervading countless worlds. His demeanor was upright and proper, the characteristics and marks of his body were especially marvelous, and his hands always gave forth inexhaustible treasures, raiment, food and drink, wonderful flowers and incense, images, banners, and [other] implements of exceeding splendor. In such matters he surpasses all *devas* and humans, and he has attained complete ease in all *dharmas*.[38]

---

[38] The citation, beginning from the first set of quotation marks, is found at T12n0360_p0269c10–270a02 with some variation. Taixu shortened and paraphrased the lead-in to this citation, so I have left the first phrase outside of the quotation marks.

Ah! The Pure Land in the Human Realm! We should set forth compassionate vows and move forward making offerings, seeking [the goal] with diligence and bringing all manner of beings across the ford. Here I append a poem that says:

What world is this present world?
A hell within the human realm!
One should make compassionate vows
to abandon [even] body, life, and wealth.
Advancing virtues in peoples' minds,
and vow to purify a buddha-land.
The Three Treasures will uphold you.
Hail to the Tathāgata![39]

(Distributed by Buddhist Studies Publishing Company)

Appendix: "Creating the Pure Land in the Human Realm" (*Chuangzao renjian jingtu* 刱造人間淨土)

Lecture delivered in November 1930

(425) Since I have been travelling in the hot springs public park and looking around at your esteemed locale's new construction on the hospitality of Mr. Lu Zuofu, I have had the opportunity to chat with all of you, and for this I am most grateful. Just now Mr. Lu brought up "Taixu's Progress in History," meaning [my] efforts at reforming Buddhism itself and causing it to flourish throughout the entire world, and this has certainly been Taixu's aspiration. So far, however, I am acutely embarrassed to say that there has been nothing by way of actual results, so it all seems like nothing more than empty talk. But now, upon seeing your esteemed office's new buildings that "do away with the old to make way for the new" and "turn the defiled into the pure,"[40] I would like to bring up the topic of "Creating the Pure Land in the Human Realm" and have a discussion with you about it.

First, the Pure Land described in Buddhist studies points to a kind of good society or a beautiful world. The word "land" (*tu* 土) means a "country" (*guotu* 國土; Skt. *kṣetra*), and it indicates a world (*shijie* 世界). Generally, all the people,

---

[39] According to Dr. Jonathan Chaves, this summative verse consists of snippets of poems and songs from various eras. Taixu brought them together in a way that put the final exhortation of this essay into an easily-memorized verse. E-mail correspondence, July 3, 2018.
[40] The phrases *ge gu ding xin* 革故鼎新 and *zhuan hui wei jing* 轉穢為淨 appear several times in Buddhist literature, so I imagine that Taixu is quoting them as commonplaces.

things, and images in this world are stately, pure, exquisite, and good, and thus it is regarded as a pure land. The pure lands referred to in the Buddhist canon are posited in opposition to our present defiled world. The world in which we live, filled with impurity and evil, is considered the evil world of the Five Defilements:

If the times are bad and filled with upheavals, this is called the defilement of the *kalpa* (*jiezhuo* 劫濁). When views are heterodox and false views arise easily, this is called the defilement of views (*jianzhuo* 見濁). When people do not get what they want and they experience worries and vexations, this is called the defilement of affliction (*fannaozhuo* 煩惱濁). When humans and animals act more in evil ways than good, this is called the defilement of sentient beings (*zhongshengzhuo* 眾生濁). When few reach the age of 100, this is called the defilement of lifespan (*mingzhuo* 命濁). This present world has all these five defilements, and human beings mostly practice evil. Therefore, it is not a pure land.

A pure land [by contrast] refers to the various pure lands that lie beyond this world, such as the western Pure Land of Utmost Bliss or the eastern Pure Land of Lapis Lazuli.[41] These are seen as pure and stately superior lands. According to modern astronomy, there are many stars and worlds beyond this Earth (426), and there must be some that are both worse and better than this one. This suffices to prove that there could be a superior pure land beyond this world. Thus, a comparison shows that this human realm is not a pure land, and observing that this human realm is a defiled land with many deficiencies reveals the nature of all the pure lands in other places.

But after Buddhist learning has explained pure lands by means of comparison, it goes on to explain the causes and conditions through which a pure land is established. A pure land does not just come about spontaneously, nor is it created by a deity. It comes about by the arousal of good within the minds of sentient beings such as humans, which leads them to seek after clear and definite knowledge, which gives rise to correct thoughts and engagement in all kinds of reasoned action. By persevering in correct behavior without interruption they produce all kinds of good karma. The end result will be the achievement of a good society and an exquisite world.

In this way the Buddhist scriptures give very clear answers to questions about the manner in which pure lands originate and become realities. Everything from each plant and tree right up to every star and sun comes into being when

---

[41] There are no references to this Pure Land under this name in any CBETA text. However, Bhaiṣajyaguru Buddha is given as the resident *tathāgata* in the *Fo shuo beidou qixing yanming jing* 佛說北斗七星延命經 (T.1307). See T21n1307_p0426a13–a14.

countless causes and conditions work together. The starting point is the power of the mind of every sentient being such as humans. The power of mind lies in each kind of thought, knowledge, and so on and their engagement in each kind of study and each kind of activity. After long accumulation, the causes are complete and their fruits ripen either as a good society or as a purified and stately land.

Returning now to the narrower scope of China, its undeveloped economic power, slumping social enterprises, citizens' debates and polemics, and governmental disarray make it seem nothing but an ugly country of defilement and evil. Compared with this, the happier situation of the Americans seems like a pure land. However, China (427) became a defiled land because the minds of people in former times were not correct. Conversely, if people today could apply their minds to good and bring forth pure thoughts, and if they exert themselves in setting up all forms of legitimate enterprise, then how hard would it be to turn this impure and evil China into a Chinese pure land?

Second, what is the Pure Land in the Human Realm? These days, most practitioners of Pure Land believe that the present land is defiled and that they must leave this evil, turbid world and seek rebirth in another, better land that is pure. But this is part of the Hinayana teaching on benefitting oneself and not the Mahayana way of practicing Pure Land. This is like some people who believe that China's environment is not optimal and that they have to leave in order to pursue their dreams, at the same time pining for America as a land of plenty and pleasure. Because of this, they up and leave China, seek American citizenship, and learn to think like Americans. All of this comes from being weak-willed or not really understanding the rationale behind Pure Land. But all things arise always and everywhere from the transformations within varieties of conditions, and if one traces these transformations back to their source, then [one finds that] the starting point for all of them is the mental motive forces of all humans and other sentient beings. Since all people have this power of mind, they all have the inherent ability to create a pure land, and they can all make vows to bring about its successful creation in this world. If they put forth the effort and get to it, they can create a pure land here in this human realm, and there is no need to leave this [supposedly] filthy society and go seek a pure society elsewhere. To be blunt, even if this present land is neither good nor stately, if everyone would work to purify their own minds and cultivate themselves so as to accumulate pure and virtuous causes and conditions, then step by step, for however long it takes, this defiled and evil human realm can be transformed into a magnificent pure land. There is no need to leave this human realm and look for a pure land somewhere else. This is why it is called "the Pure Land in the Human Realm."

(428) Third, why should we want to create it? The Pure Land in the Human Realm as described above is something that we must create. Therefore, we have to do away with the misunderstandings of the pessimists and the optimists. The pessimists believe this present human world cannot be turned into a pure land and it's better either to commit suicide or just drift through life. There's no point in making any effort. The optimists think that the present world of humanity is already a wondrous pure land. They are infatuated with the way things are and do not seek any further progress. We need to break through the preconceived ideas of these two groups and show them that everything in the world arises from causes and conditions beginning in the minds of all human and [other] sentient beings. When the mind is not peaceful and pure, the end result will not be a pure land. If the mind is peaceful and pure, then it can provide the initial impetus for creating a pure land.

They also need to understand that all things arise from causes and conditions, and so [the views of] creation by a deity, materialism, and idealism are all wrong. The power of the mind is nothing more than the primary director among conditions, like a leader coming forth from the populace. This is the real principle behind the creation of a pure land, but it needs to come about through an intellectual revolution to uproot erroneous thinking and nurture the confluence of right principles with thoughts and consciousness to bring them into fullest play. It is just like when the latest discoveries of science validate the true principles of Buddhist teachings. During the past nineteen centuries, science held that all the things in the world were composed of atoms as their fundamental building blocks. The newest science of the twentieth century has shown that all things in the world have no ultimate basis, but that each and every one arises from the confluence of a multitude of causes and conditions as they interrelate under various circumstances. This comes very near to Buddhist teachings. Thus, the rationale for creating a Pure Land in the Human Realm according to Buddhist teachings is gradually gaining (429) the approbation of the latest science, and [science] could well bring it up directly.

In sum, the present human world is far from perfect, but if human and other sentient beings are willing to go and create a pure land, it would not be impossible. All that is needed is to put aside preconceived notions and then put forth reasonable efforts to create it!

Fourth, how do we go about creating it? Human effort can create the Pure Land in the Human Realm, but how will they do it? The Pure Land in the

Human Realm first needs people to conceive the notion to create it, and once they do, then [it requires] these practical steps: First, the government has to make a concrete contribution. It is like when we hear that there is a bandit lair in the area. For the local rulers to build something new, they must first rely on defense forces to root out the entrenched evil powers with military power. Firmly holding on to the political authority needed to manage public affairs, they can use the laws to mete out rewards and punishments and build things up systematically. Thus, the government is the overall pivot for establishing [the Pure Land in the Human Realm].

However, implementation requires a division of labor. First comes industry. Once industry is developed, then the basic necessities of life such as clothing, food, housing, and mobility will be assured. Second comes education. Education transforms thought and increases [peoples'] capabilities. Education must advance so that society can advance. Third, the arts. The arts can raise industry up, and from this it can advance to the fine arts which bring pleasure and enjoyment, lift spirits, and gladden our nature. Its effect is to elevate our thought and make us whole in body and mind. Fourth, morals. Morals are at the root of education, bringing [mere] guidance in the acquisition of knowledge to a level of moral guidance and advancing self-restraint, good faith, and the practice of self-rectification, and it can stabilize the good society over the long haul (430). Never neglect the creative mind to sustain development and seek further progress. As German sociology of knowledge has it, there are three kinds of knowledge in the world: modern Western scientific knowledge, industrial and other merely practical [sorts of] knowledge, and relatively amoral knowledge for building oneself up. China and Athens had philosophers who stressed virtuous conduct as their main point, along with which one may add Buddhism as representative of practices for liberation.

Second, therefore, we should rely upon the spirit of Buddhist teachings as the ultimate place of refuge. As stated above, government in all its functions can go a long way, but its potential still has limits. In order to take these limits and push them to the limitless, one must look to Buddhism. Buddhism unites all of humanity in the cosmos into one, could constitute the creation and advancement of the Pure Land in the Human Realm, and aid progress toward morals, which is the first step in Mahayana bodhisattva practice. Take this as the foundation and keep making efforts over an unlimited period of time without interruption, and there will be forward progress toward a Buddha-cosmos. From this it will become apparent that each individual belongs to the entire cosmos, and the entire cosmos belongs to each individual. There is not one thing one could bring up that would not be like this, on account of which everything becomes limitless without exceeding its limits. With fierce and energetic effort over a long span of time the Pure Land will be achieved, and with it the prediction of non-retrogression!

Part Three

The Pure Land in the Human Realm after Taixu and Conclusions

7

The Pure Land in the Human Realm after Taixu

After Taixu coined it, the phrase "Pure Land in the Human Realm" entered the vocabulary of Chinese Buddhism, but its meaning has never been fixed. It has proved a very elastic term that can signify many things, and Taixu's successors have used it or related terms to encapsulate their own variations on Taixu's ideas. Some remain close to his vision, while others use it to strike out in other directions.

We will begin by noting that all the new usages of the "Pure Land in the Human Realm" differ from Taixu's in one significant way. As noted in Chapter 2, Taixu formulated this concept a few years before he began using the term "Buddhism for Human Life." Thus, at the time he wrote the Essay the term "Pure Land in the Human Realm" was not subordinate to a larger framework for revisioning Buddhism. The reverse is true for all later thinkers. "Buddhism for Human Life" or "Buddhism for the Human Realm" provides the overall scheme within which the construction of a Pure Land in the Human Realm forms one component.

Yinshun

Ven. Yinshun (印順, 1906–2005) studied in Taixu's Buddhist seminaries and edited Taixu's chronological biography (*nianpu* 年譜) and *Complete Works*. While he continued to use Taixu's concept of "Buddhism for Human Life" (*rensheng fojiao* 人生佛教) or "Buddhism for the Human Realm" (*renjian fojiao* 人間佛教),[1] he was not the active reformer that Taixu had been. Rather, he was a

---

[1] There is a body of scholarship which holds that Taixu used the term "Buddhism for Human Life" in order to point Buddhists away from services to the dead and toward the living, while Yinshun deliberately changed the term to "Buddhism for the Human Realm" in order to reorient Buddhists from a focus on offerings to ghosts and deities to, again, service within the human domain (see, for

scholar trying to recover the history of Indian Buddhism for a Chinese audience. Because Yinshun considered early Indian Mahayana thought normative and later Chinese developments inauthentic, he kept his focus on Indian materials and did not take Chinese texts and traditions as his basis to the extent Taixu had (Travagnin 2004, 275). In fact, he saw Pure Land as a Chinese debasement of Indian Buddhism.

Thus, when he used the term "Pure Land in the Human Realm," he tended to be descriptive rather than prescriptive. Specifically, he identified it as one of three ways of thinking about the Pure Land in Indian sources alongside the ideas of "the Pure Land of Rebirth" (*wangsheng jingtu* 往生淨土) and "the Pure Land That One Arrays" (*zhuangyan jingtu* 莊嚴淨土). The "Pure Land of Rebirth" referred to traditional Chinese ideas about gaining entry into a pure buddha-land to whose creation one had contributed nothing. The "Pure Land That One Arrays" pointed to the way in which bodhisattvas on their way to buddhahood made vows in order to lay out a plan for the creation of the buddha-land that they would eventually inhabit, as Amitābha had done with his forty-eight vows. This idea emphasized the active role that a practitioner could take in creating a pure land rather than the passive stance that one assumed by seeking nothing more than rebirth in an already-created land. Finally, the "Pure Land in the Human Realm" brought to a focus the manner in which present human practitioners cooperated with buddhas and bodhisattvas in continually making and inhabiting a Pure Land (Yinshun 1992, 125–6; Travagnin 2004, 306).

Thus, it seems Yinshun concerned himself primarily with the practitioner's choice between two of the three types of pure land, the "Pure Land of Rebirth" and "the Pure Land that One Arrays." Where did the third type, the "Pure Land in the Human Realm," fit into his scheme? In the chapter entitled "Types of Pure Lands" (*jingtu de leibie* 淨土的類別) in the "New Treatise on Pure Land" (*Jingtu xin lun* 淨土新論) chapter of his book *Jingtu yu chan* 淨土與禪 (Pure Land and Chan), he speaks of it in only one of the senses that Taixu had employed in the Essay. It refers narrowly to this Earth once Maitreya has descended from the Tuṣita Heaven and achieved buddhahood (Yinshun 1992a, 5–6). Later, when specifically discussing the "Pure Land of Maitreya," Yinshun notes that only when Maitreya has become a buddha here on Earth will the human realm achieve purity; later Buddhists distorted this teaching by claiming that the Tuṣita Heaven itself was a pure land and seeking rebirth there. This is wrong, and

example, Yang 1991). Others point out that Taixu used both terms and the difference between them does not really amount to much. Even Yang Huinan 楊惠南 agrees to this (Yang 1991, 122–3).

degrades proper Maitreya devotion into just another passive desire for rebirth in a pure realm. If one aspires to rebirth in the Tuṣita Heaven, it should be only so that one may follow Maitreya when he becomes a buddha in his following life and, by his presence, renders this world pure (Yinshun 1992a, 16–20).

He does not discuss the idea of the Pure Land in the Human Realm much beyond this, and we must conclude that it was not central to his own program of reformulating Chinese Buddhism. Thus, while Taixu could be quite expansive about ways of instantiating the Pure Land in the Human Realm by seeking rebirth in Uttarakuru, pursuing technological innovations, and promoting social justice in addition to accompanying Maitreya on his path to buddhahood, for Yinshun the concept applied only to this last goal.

Yinshun did not gain much support for his ideas because the tone of his writings on Pure Land struck many traditionalists as highly antagonistic (see Jones 1999, 125–33). In addition, he wrote as a historian making pronouncements on Buddhist history and not as a monk leading a movement or a pastor exhorting individuals to vigorous spiritual practice. Nevertheless, he transmitted the idea of the "Pure Land in the Human Realm" to disciples who did work more closely with modern practicing Buddhists.

Xingyun

Ven. Xingyun (星雲, 1927–), the founder of the Foguang Shan 佛光山 complex in Taiwan and the Buddha's Light International Association, has also adopted the term "Pure Land in the Human Realm," and he explains it in much the same way that Taixu did. That is, he discourages his followers from taking a passive stance toward social problems while awaiting rebirth in Sukhāvatī (or any other Buddhist paradise). Instead, he instructs them to work toward the resolution of social problems while trusting that their devotion to Amitābha will bring about rebirth in the Pure Land after death. Hearkening back to Taixu's juxtaposition of Uttarakuru as a paradise into which one may gain birth with a future world in which people produce Uttarakuru's splendors through technology, Xingyun teaches that achievement of an ideal world will happen in three stages. In the first stage, people will use new technologies to replicate the *deva*-realms where gods live in comfort and bliss (Xingyun thus substitutes the *deva*-realms for Uttarakuru). The second will see the transformation of this world into a buddha-land, at which time the resolution of social and environmental problems achieved in this and the previous stage will be crowned by enlightenment and buddhahood. Once this happens, then in the third stage this very world will appear as the Lotus-calyx world of the *Huayan Sutra* (Chandler 2004, 47–56) that recalls Taixu's description of the "Pure Land of the Ocean of Awakening." Like Taixu before him, Xingyun sought to blend traditional Pure Land practices and cosmology with modern social and political concerns.

While Xingyun's ideas about the Pure Land in the Human Realm resemble those of Taixu in many respects, he also put his own individual stamp on the concept. Most notably, he coined a new term: the Foguang (or Buddha's Light) Pure Land (*Foguang jingtu* 佛光淨土), which he defined in the following way:

> The Foguang Pure Land is a "World transformed by Buddhism" (*fohua de shijie* 佛化的世界): Each individual person takes refuge in the Three Jewels, accepts and keeps the Five Lay Precepts, is clear about causes and is cognizant of effects, and establishes friendly relations with all.
>
> The Foguang Pure Land is a "World of goodness and beauty" (*shanmei de shijie* 善美的世界): What everyone sees, hears, says and does is unfailingly virtuous and lovely.
>
> The Foguang Pure Land is a "World of Peace and Bliss" (*anle de shijie* 安樂的世界): Each person's relationship with others will have no envy, only respect; no hatred, only warmth; no avarice, only generosity; and no detriment, only success.
>
> The Foguang Pure Land is a "World of Joy" (*xiyue de shijie* 喜悅的世界): It will be pleasant and beautiful at all times, and all places will be domains of ultimate wisdom. (Xingyun 2008a, 3:313)

At one level, his mountain complex at Foguang Shan instantiated this ideal: "As far as Foguang Shan is concerned, I feel that our present temple complex should give followers deep faith—then it is the western Pure Land, and we can give people peace and nurturance" (Xingyun 2008, 547).[2] However, this was just the beginning. In a manner reminiscent of Taixu's follower Zang Guanchan's (藏貫禪) dream of an international Buddhist organization planting intentional communities in several countries, Foguang Shan and the Buddha's Light International Association have satellite communities around the world. These help to spread the ideal of the Foguang Pure Land.

Xingyun saw his formulation of the Foguang Pure Land as especially advantageous. While he did not deny the validity of earlier Buddhist formulations of Pure Land doctrine and practice, he believed they all suffered from one

---

[2] All the quotations from Xingyun's works herein were found in Chen (Forthcoming).

shortcoming or another, which his teaching on the Foguang Pure Land avoided by combining all their best features. It would

> combine the pure environment and unity of all into one household [found in] the Pure Land of Amitābha; the clean government and abundant livelihood of the Pure Land of Medicine Buddha; the mutual friendship and harmonious equality of the Lotus-Calyx Pure Land; the ingathering of virtuous people and inexhaustible joy in the Dharma of the Tuṣita Pure Land in order to turn this impure Human Realm into the Foguang Pure Land. (Xingyun 2008a, 3:310)

In sum, the Pure Land in the Human Realm, rebranded as the "Foguang Pure Land," would come about progressively as more and more people came to take refuge in Buddhism and adopt its virtues and disciplines. Far from being a product of secular technological advances or individual cultivation aimed at world-transcendence, it would be the result of widespread conversion and reform that would yield a better world here and now.

Sheng Yen

Perhaps none of Taixu's modern successors has carried forward his thoughts about the Pure Land in the Human Realm in all its complexity as much as Sheng Yen (*Shengyan* 聖嚴, 1930–2009) has. Sheng Yen has written theoretical works on Pure Land, but here I will focus on a book edited from his dharma-talks entitled *Shengyan fashi jiao jingtu famen* 聖嚴法師教淨土法門 (*Master Sheng Yen Teaches the Pure Land Dharma-Gate*), which brings together transcripts of talks given to participants in a seven-day Buddha-recitation retreat (*foqi* 佛七). On reading these transcripts, one notices that he follows Taixu in adopting an eclectic approach that excludes nothing. Far from using the idea of the Pure Land in the Human Realm to supersede the ideas and practices of the past, he finds ways to fit all these elements together: *nianfo* to gain rebirth in Sukhāvatī through the power of Amitābha's vows, efforts in self-cultivation in order to make as much personal progress as possible, affirmation that the Pure Land is a manifestation of the mind, and benevolent work in the present world to create a Pure Land here and now. In addition, while Taixu moved from one of these elements to another seemingly at random, Sheng Yen attempts to systematize them into a more coherent whole.

Sheng Yen begins by asserting that there is no inherent conflict between believing that the Pure Land exists literally to the west and the possibility of the "Pure Land in the Human Realm" (Sheng Yen 2010, 88). This is because the practice of Humanistic Buddhism (*renjian fojiao* 人間佛教) does not conflict with the aspiration for rebirth in Amitābha's land; in fact, it prepares one for it (Sheng Yen 2010, 89). In asserting this, Sheng Yen implicitly repudiates prior critics who held that the wish to attain rebirth in the Pure Land is "otherworldly" (*chushi* 出世) and arises from a loss of hope for this world. In contrast, he states that all Mahayana Buddhists ought to generate *bodhicitta*, which entails the desire to save all other beings. When one has this attitude, then one accords with the vows set forth by all buddhas, which Amitābha's forty-eight vows exemplify. Normatively, one should vow *both* to bring about the Pure Land in the Human Realm by assisting living beings in the present world *and* seek rebirth in Sukhāvatī after death. In this way, one gains a higher rebirth in the Pure Land, becomes a buddha sooner, and can get about the business of aiding suffering beings more quickly (Sheng Yen 2010, 90–3). Later, Sheng Yen states that the Pure Land is not inherently otherworldly and escapist; to the contrary, escapism and passivity toward the problems of the world are signs of an unbalanced understanding of Pure Land (Sheng Yen 2010, 111).

While thus denying any conflict between a traditional "western-direction" idea of the Pure Land and social action in the present world, Sheng Yen also sought to harmonize the more traditional dichotomy between "western-direction" and "mind-only" Pure Land just as Taixu did when discussing the "Pure Land of the Ocean of Awakening." In the course of counseling retreatants to engage in all the traditional Buddhist methods of self-cultivation, Sheng Yen mentions that, in keeping with the principle of mind-only (*weixin* 唯心), every Pure Land is only as pure as the mind experiencing it. To a buddha, even this defiled Sahā world presents itself as utterly pure (Sheng Yen 2010, 162). The Pure Land is a kind of "one-room schoolhouse" in which students from various grades inhabit the same space but only receive such instruction as their prior experience has prepared them. This does not falsify the "western-direction" concept; if that is what a particular being is ready to receive, then it will be given and will be as real as any other experience to an unenlightened mind. Even so, such beings *will* be in the Pure Land and will attain buddhahood. Sheng Yen goes so far as to speculate that there may be as many Pure Lands as there are minds (Sheng Yen 2010, 163).

He also systematically relates mind-only Pure Land with the call for social action to create a Pure Land in the present human world. To begin with, he downplays the value of a strict "mind-only" position by saying that if purification of one's own mind were the way to establish a Pure Land here and now, then only those who have so purified their minds would be able to perceive and dwell in it; all others would be left out. Should we then try to establish a Pure Land within the family or in a given territory? Perhaps, he says. Since the Buddha seemed to think this present world was the best place for practice, then it would be worth a try (Sheng Yen 2003, 24). The founding of Dharma Drum Mountain (*Fagu shan* 法鼓山) in Taiwan represents his own attempt. While at first glance it might seem that Sheng Yen is trying to carry out Taixu's plan for an ideal Buddhist community on a mountain, Sheng Yen's rationale is more modest and practical. In remarks given at a 1997 conference, he described three main goals that, if accomplished, would go some distance in establishing Dharma Drum Mountain as a Pure Land in the Human Realm:

1. He planned for several educational institutions on the property that would teach religion and the humanities to help both Buddhism and society.
2. He planned an office to organize outreach and publication efforts for the uplift of society.
3. He would also make provisions to educate the general population in social concern and social work. (Sheng Yen 2003, 151)

To summarize, Sheng Yen presents a more concise and coherent scheme than Taixu's rather eclectic conception of the Pure Land in the Human Realm. Sheng Yen omitted many of the elements found in Taixu's Essay (e.g., rebirth in Uttarakuru[3] and government-sponsored Buddhist utopias), and took the three elements of Pure Land previously assumed to be mutually antagonistic and brought them together. Amitābha's Pure Land as it really exists as a place in which one may attain rebirth, the pure land that appears when one's mind is pure, and the Pure Land in the Human Realm do not contradict one another; in fact, one needs all three. In isolation, the search for rebirth in Sukhāvatī is indeed escapist and otherworldly, a "mind-only Pure Land" would benefit only the one whose mind has been purified, and efforts to construct a Pure Land in the Human Realm without aspirations for rebirth and mental purification would be just another form of clinging. All three forms of Pure Land have their place even within the life and practice of an individual devotee.

---

[3] In another work, Sheng Yen does mention Uttarakuru as a kind of Pure Land in the Human Realm, but says that "regrettably there is currently no conveyance to transport us there." See Sheng Yen (2003, 23).

Other Examples

We must also notice that the phrase "Pure Land in the Human Realm" has taken on a life of its own as a floating signifier available for whatever purpose it can help advance. For example, in a 1998 essay called "The Pure Land in the Human Realm from a Feminist Perspective" (*Cong nüxing zhuyi jiaodu kan renjian jingtu* 從女性主義角度看人間淨土) the scholar Mei Naiwen 梅迺文 wrote:

> The ideal of the Pure Land in the Human Realm is to bring the Pure Land of Buddhism down into the human world and establish an ideal land within the human domain. However, the human domain comprises both the male and female genders, and if it lacks the full support and participation of one of the sexes, then it will be impossible to achieve the Pure Land in the Human Realm. This "full support and participation" must obtain at all levels, with no limitations accruing from gender, religion, economics, education, society, or government. (Mei 1998, 151)

The remainder of the essay lays out the author's requirements for implementing gender equality in present-day society, with no attempt to relate this program to rebirth in Amitābha's or Maitreya's pure lands. The Pure Land in the Human Realm seemingly functions as a way of relating the end goal of a social movement to Buddhism.

In the early 1990s, a group of progressive Buddhists in Taiwan launched a magazine called *Buddhist Culture* (*Fojiao wenhua* 佛教文化), the purpose of which was to help bring about the Pure Land in the Human Realm. As the editor, Li Zhenglong 李政隆 explained in the inaugural editorial, Buddhism in the past had displayed a passive attitude toward social problems, while Christianity had entered China building hospitals, orphanages, and soup kitchens. This had led people to say, "The more places there are that people hold to orthodox Buddhism, the more poverty and misery there will be" (*Yu shi zichi zhengxin fojiao de difang, jiu yu pinqiong tongku* 愈是自持正信佛教的地方,就愈貧窮痛苦; Li 1989, 2). In response, he argued that Buddhism espoused the practice of both fortune and wisdom (*fuhui* 福慧). When people are born, they have two kinds of power driving their existence: past karma and vows (*yuanli* 願力). The first leads one to one's present circumstance; the second charts the path for the bodhisattva going forward.

As bodhisattva practitioners, today's Buddhists should take vows to work life after life for the benefit of others. By keeping such vows together with other Buddhists, they will cause the present world to move closer and closer to the future in which Maitreya will descend, attain buddhahood, and turn this very human world into a Pure Land. However, the fruits of this practice do not appear only in this distant future; the cooperation of multitudes of Mahayana Buddhists carrying out bodhisattva vows in concert will turn even the present world into a pure place of practice, and the Pure Land in the Human Realm can appear here and now. Thus, he says, the new magazine's purpose will be to call Buddhists to exert themselves to the utmost to "bring Buddhism into life, bring compassion into society" (*fojiao shenghuohua, beixin shehuihua* 佛教生活化，悲心社會化), and thus create a pure land in the human world (Li 1989, 2).

In the opening editorial of the first numbered issue, Li takes on a commonly cited quotation from the *Vimalakīrti Sūtra* to the effect that "when the mind is pure, the buddha-land will be pure" (*xin jing ji guotu jing* 心淨即國土淨; T14n0475_p0538c06, see Watson 1997, 29). This is shorthand for a belief long held in China that the present world is inherently pure, and that its perceived impurity is merely a projection of impure minds (see Jones 2019, 41–3). This is the position that Taixu has labeled as overly optimistic in his Essay, since it held that there is actually nothing wrong or impure about the world and thus no work to be done to improve it; individual mental purification will accomplish all that is needful. Li's concern here is similar: holding this belief will vitiate any motivation for Buddhists to work on behalf of society or the environment. He says, "People who hold this belief will claim that this very world is a Pure Land no matter how bad its environment is" (Li 1990, 2). Next Li excoriates the very view that Taixu held to be too pessimistic: Suffering is inherent to the nature of this world, and so any effort to salvage it is doomed. One's only hope is to perform *nianfo* and escape to the Pure Land of Amitābha after death (Li 1990, 2). Thus, while Li does not mention Taixu by name, the latter's influence is unmistakable.

To counter the passivity that follows from both attitudes, Li follows Yinshun in pointing out that buddhas arise from within the human realm, and they do so by taking and keeping bodhisattva vows life after life, working tirelessly for the welfare of all. The remainder of the editorial repeats the points made in the inaugural issue, but this issue follows up by reporting on a symposium attended by several scholar-practitioners on the topic of creating the Pure Land in the Human Realm (Li et al. 1990, 10–16). While the discussion demonstrates some variety among the views of the participants, by and large it follows the lines laid down in the two preceding editorials. In sum, they recognize that, as Buddhists, they affirm the doctrine of rebirth and aver that modern Buddhists should take bodhisattva vows whose effects will last beyond their present lives and will entail ceaseless efforts in serving the world in which they live, neither passing off its impurity and suffering as a mere mental projection nor giving up and pinning all hope on rebirth in Amitābha's Pure Land after death. They also affirm the belief that the Pure Land in the Human Realm is a *telos* that will be realized when Maitreya attains buddhahood on this Earth in the future, but which is also proleptically present as more and more bodhisattvas join their efforts to purify the world and mitigate suffering. While Taixu and Yinshun are not named in the discussion, echoes of their thought are clearly present, although the emphasis on reform work in the present world exceeds theirs. In addition, the view that present welfare work brings out *in nuce* the Pure Land that will only be fully realized in the days of Maitreya's descent echoes Tang Dayuan's teaching on the "new Pure Land" more than Taixu's "Pure Land in the Human Realm."

Mainland China

All of the examples we have examined so far come from Taiwan, where the phrase "Pure Land in the Human Realm" has moved into wide usage. It seems less important in mainland China, as can be seen by examining a general introduction to Pure Land Buddhism by Ven. Daan (大安, 1959–), a leading proponent of Pure Land in the modern People's Republic of China. In this book, the term *renjian jingtu* appears only twice. In the first instance, Daan says it is what will result when Buddhists put the various virtuous practices of the *Contemplation Sutra* into operation: honoring parents, serving teachers, compassionately refraining from killing, and practicing the Ten Virtues. If these are implemented to such an extent that they lift up all of society, then we may call this the Pure Land in the Human Realm (Daan 2006, 47). The second reference, found much later in the text, merely repeats this idea (Daan 2006, 537). In both cases the term appears without elaboration, serving as an offhand remark or slogan and not developed as a programmatic element.

Perhaps we see the most striking example of the elasticity of the term "Pure Land in the Human Realm" in its co-option by the Chinese Communist Party (CCP) as a way to marshal Buddhist support for some of its social and cultural campaigns. Because Taixu enjoyed a close working relationship with the Nationalist Party (*Guomindang* 國民黨) during the last decades of his life, CCP discourse banned his name but occasionally made use of his ideas. For example, the Great Leap Forward, mobilization for the Korean War, and the Land Reform movements were promoted in many ways, including a promise that it would bring about the "Pure Land in the Human Realm" or "Sukhāvatī on Earth" (*renjian jile shijie* 人間極樂世界) among other Buddhist-tinged slogans (Ji 2013, 37–8). When the CCP permitted the Buddhist Association of China to resume officially sanctioned Buddhist activities in the early 1960s under party supervision, its first chairman, Zhao Puchu 趙樸初 (1907–2000), adopted the general framework of Humanistic Buddhism and the goal of establishing the Pure Land in the Human Realm as general indicators, again without mentioning Taixu by name (Ji 2013, 39–50). For Zhao, this was the way to build a "socialist spiritual civilization" that fully accorded with the aims of the party.

In 1926, Taixu was concerned about taking the very traditional form of Buddhist practice and keeping it relevant in a world that seemed to be veering rapidly toward scientism and secular politics. His Essay brims over with sutra quotations and counsels to traditional practices while arguing that these things are compatible with modern life. Most of his successors took over the slogan "Build the Pure Land in the Human Realm" but emptied it of most of its meaning, keeping it only as a way to talk about Buddhist-motivated social action or as a sign to post at the entrance of a Buddhist temple or center. Xingyun and Sheng Yen kept Taixu's spirit of accommodation of the traditional and the modern intact, and they lived to see times calm enough for them to think carefully about the components they would need to assemble to make it work. The editorial board of *Buddhist Culture* maintained some of the traditional elements in Taixu's Essay, but stayed closer to Yinshun's more modest construction with a modicum of Tang's metaphysics. In all cases, the idea of the Pure Land in the Human Realm, whether serving as a comprehensive program or simply as a slogan, has demonstrated its staying power up to the present.

8

Concluding Remarks

I have approached Taixu's Essay not as a student of Buddhism in Republican-period China, but as a scholar of Chinese Pure Land Buddhism. In this connection, Taixu's proposal for the establishment of a "Pure Land in the Human Realm" represented an advance over the centuries-long opposition between the visions of a Pure Land that existed concretely to the west of our defiled world and of a Pure Land that manifests when one purifies one's mind and sees the present world correctly. As I have noted elsewhere (Jones 2019, ch. 3), neither of these ideas suited Chinese modernizers. The first idea corresponds to the point of view that Taixu labeled as too pessimistic in his Essay, since it gave up on this world and sought escape to a pure buddha-land. The other he considered too optimistic, as it taught that there is nothing inherently wrong with the present world, and thus no need to expend any effort in reforming it. Neither of these formulations provided a warrant for the hard work of improving present conditions.

Taixu charted a course between rank pessimism and rosy optimism by encouraging his followers to work for reform in the present world and make it a "pure land," but without giving up their identities as Buddhists as the more secular modernizers would have preferred. At the same time, they did not have to give up on either the previous "western direction" or "mind-only" constructs that had dominated Pure Land polemics in previous eras. Neither was inherently incompatible with working for improvement here and now. This innovation imparted a new forward impetus to a form of Buddhist practice that had not seen any advances for a very long time. This deserves recognition.

One of the reasons the concept of building the Pure Land in the Human Realm worked was that in it Taixu combined the notions of paradises and utopias as detailed in Chapter 4. Traditionally, Pure Land thought conceived of Amitābha's Land of Bliss as a paradise, that is, as an ideal environment that humans can access but have no part in planning or implementing. Secular modernizers, in contrast, gave great thought to establishing utopias, realms made ideal through human efforts in technological advancement, political theory, and social engineering. In the past, paradisiacal and utopian thinking tended toward opposition. Utopian thinkers saw paradises as distracting dreamscapes, imaginary creations of people who had given up all hope in this world and just wanted out. Those who favored paradises thought of utopians as overly optimistic about the human capacity for fulfilling common needs, and were always making grand plans that either fell short of expectations or were perverted into evil paths. For utopians, paradises were passive and boring, while for those dreaming of a paradise, utopias were potentially coercive and authoritarian.

Taixu, by combining both approaches, sought to overcome the problems inherent in each. By retaining goals that met the description of paradises, such as Sukhāvatī, Uttarakuru, or the Inner Court of Maitreya, he provided not only a postmortem hope that endured beyond death and gave meaning to one's life even in a present utopia, but which also overcame passivity and boredom by providing a religious vision that one could pursue even as one worked to establish a utopia. By also affirming the possibility that social reform, political restructuring, and technological development could provide a utopia here and now, he gave people a reason to engage the world. He astutely observed that one could work toward both goals, and that the effort one expended toward one also assisted in the attainment of the other. The work one did to establish a utopia in the present world, if based on the Buddhist motivation of bodhisattva compassion, would actually help one to gain rebirth in a paradise after death inevitably ended one's activism. Even then, one's journey continued to the final goal of buddhahood and mastery of skillful means. As we have seen, Taixu's successors, notably Sheng Yen, have maintained this dual emphasis.

For this plan to work, it had to be grounded both in traditional Buddhism and in modernist thinking. Otherwise, Taixu would have been simply another Buddhist conservative or one more secular modernist. Making the two work together, however, was not always easy, and it led Taixu into eclecticism and inconsistency. For example, even as he disagreed with secular modernists such as Chen Duxiu that science must eradicate religion by claiming Buddhism as a higher form of empiricism, he did not always think through what that would mean in practice. Traditional Buddhist cosmology, upon which the very existence of the Land of Bliss, Uttarakuru, and the Inner Court of the Tuṣita Heaven make sense, did not comport well with the findings of modern astronomy in 1926, and one cannot overcome the difficulty by remarking off-handedly that perhaps Uttarakuru is just another planet in our solar system.

Nevertheless, once we understand that Taixu was not just a modernizer in a Western secularist mode, then much of what he wrote in the Essay makes more sense. As we noted above, interlocutors and scholars tended to explain away Taixu's inclusion of traditional Pure Land thought and esoteric ritual magic in his program by asserting that he was not sincere about it. They assumed he merely tossed in these elements to pander to the ignorant masses who wanted Pure Land practice and the segment of the intelligentsia who were fascinated by tantra. But long before writing his Essay, he had already classified Pure Land and Esoteric Buddhism as two of the eight schools of Chinese Buddhism. He practiced Maitreya devotionalism and aspired to rebirth in the Inner Court. He had sought supernatural powers and continued to hold out their possibility long into his reformist phase. He corrected interviewers who said that Pure Land practice was not legitimate. He cited sutras at great length, sometimes without further comment, as sufficient warrants for his plans and ideas. All this indicates that he embraced these traditional practices and goals as integral parts of his program of fitting the traditional with the modern.

Having a complete translation of Taixu's Essay in hand brings all of this into clearer view. With it, one sees the very prominent place he gives to the support of Buddhist scriptures in making his case, his wholehearted endorsement of traditional practices aimed at gaining rebirth in paradises situated squarely within a premodern Buddhist cosmos, and his desire that esoteric ritual take its rightful place alongside social activism and technological progress as a way of addressing present problems. In light of this, scholars can no longer repeat without evidence the canard that Taixu actively discouraged people from performing *nianfo* and seeking rebirth in the Pure Land of Amitābha so that they could focus their energies on social reform and political engagement.

Final Thoughts

Many years ago, John McRae published a study of the life of Eisai (or Yōsai 栄西, 1141–1215) in which he cautioned that when scholars see him only as the founder of the Japanese Rinzai Zen school, they will have difficulty accounting for other aspects of his life and work (McRae 1992, 342–5). When we see him only from the perspective of the later history of Rinzai, we have trouble understanding his interest in esoteric ritual, monastic discipline, temple architecture, and the other non-Zen aspects of his work. If we set aside his retrospective recognition as the founder of Rinzai, however, and immerse ourselves in the totality of his thought, then we can form a more coherent picture of him.

In this translation and study of one of Taixu's medium-length works, I have utilized a similar approach. From the beginning, observers saw Taixu primarily as the motive force behind the modernization of Chinese Buddhism. Indeed, when joined with the other three eminent monks of his day as the "four great monks," he became the very emblem of modernization. I argue that seeing him primarily through this lens obscured much of his thought and activities. Early interlocutors dismissed his endorsement of traditional Pure Land practice as a disingenuous concession meant only to gain support for him among ordinary Buddhists. Paul Callahan and Holmes Welch, Taixu's first two academic commentators, ignored evidence from his writings and deeds in perpetuating this image. Even today, most scholars (with the exception of Ritzinger and Zamorski) do not acknowledge how traditional much of Taixu's thought is.

As I indicated in the opening of this book, the preconception that Taixu was a modernizer and nothing else hindered my ability to absorb the contents of his Essay, and I was quite surprised to find out what it really had to say. In closing, then, I wish to leave the reader with the methodological advice that, going forward, research on Taixu needs to be based on closer readings of his corpus undertaken with a mind open to whatever we may find therein. The significance of his legacy has only grown more apparent with time, and future studies will yield progress only when they deal with the whole man in all his complexity and contradiction.

Works Cited

I. Primary Sources

Taixu's Essay

Taixu 太虛. "Jianshe renjian jingtu lun" 建設人間淨土論 ("On the Establishment of the Pure Land in the Human Realm"), in *Taixu dashi quanshu* 太虛大師全書 (The Collected Works of the Great Master Taixu), vol. 14, http://www.nanputuo.com/nptlib/html/200707/1812143485802.html.

Taixu 太虛. "Jianshe renjian jingtu lun" 建設人間淨土論 ("On the Establishment of the Pure Land in the Human Realm"), in *Taixu dashi quanshu* 太虛大師全書 (The Collected Works of the Great Master Taixu). Taipei: Shandao Temple Sutra Distribution Center 善導寺佛經流通處, 1956. vol. 24, pp. 349–430.

Other Primary Sources

Daan 大安. 2006. *Jingtu zong jiaocheng* 淨土宗教程 (A Course in Pure Land). Beijing: Zongjiao wenhua chubanshe 宗教文化出版社.

Fo shuo beidou qixing yanming jing 佛說北斗七星延命經, T.1307.

Fo shuo wuliangshou jing 佛說無量壽經, T.360.

Foshuo guan Mile pusa shangsheng doushuaitian jing 佛說觀彌勒菩薩上生兜率天經, T.452.

Giles, Lionel, trans. 1912. *Taoist Teachings from the Book of Lieh-Tzu*. London: Murray.

Inagaki Hisao and Harold Stewart, trans. 2003. *The Three Pure Land Sutras*. 2nd rev. ed. BDK English Tripitaka 12-II, III, IV. Berkeley: Numata Center for Buddhist Translation and Research.

Liu Renhang 劉仁航. 1926. *Dongfang datong xue'an* 東方大同學案 (Case Studies of Datong in the East). 2 vols. Nanjing 南京: Letian shuguan 樂天書館. Rpt: Shanghai 上海: Shanghai sanlian shudian 上海三聯書店, 2014.

Qishi yinben jing 起世因本經, T.24.

Sheng Yen 聖嚴. 2003. *Jingtu zai renjian* 淨土在人間 (The Pure Land Is in the Human Realm). Taipei: Fagu wenhua 法鼓文化.

Sheng Yen 聖嚴. 2010. *Shengyan fashi jiao jingtu famen* 聖嚴法師教淨土法門 (Master Sheng Yen Teaches the Pure Land Dharma-Gate), comp. and ed. Guoxian 果賢. Shengyan shuyuan 聖嚴書院, 5. Taipei: Fagu wenhua 法鼓文化.

Taixu. 1925. "A Statement to Asiatic Buddhists," *The Young East*, vol. 1, pp. 177–82.

Taixu. 1959. *Zhengli sengqie zhidu lun* 整理僧伽制度論 (A Proposal for Institutional Reform in the Sangha). http://www.nanputuo.com/nptlib/html/200903/2510312973499.html, accessed October 4, 2019.

Vimalakīrti Sūtra (*Weimoji suoshuo jing* 維摩詰所說經), T.475.

Watson, Burton, trans. 1997. *The Vimalakirti Sutra*. New York: Columbia University Press.

Xingyun 星雲. 2008. *Renjian fojiao xuwen xuan* 人間佛教序文選. Taipei 臺北: Xianghai wenhua shiye youxian gongsi 香海文化事業有限公司.

Xingyun 星雲. 2008a. *Renjian fojiao yulu* 人間佛教語錄. 3 vols. Taipei 臺北: Xianghai wenhua shiye youxian gongsi 香海文化事業有限公司.

Yinshun 印順, ed. 2000. *Taixu dashi nianpu* 太虛大師年譜 (Chronological Record of Great Master Taixu). Miaoyun Collection, Middle Series 妙雲集, 6. Taipei: Zhengwen Publishing Company 正聞出版社.

Zhiyi 智顗. *Miaofa lianhua jing wenju* 妙法蓮華經文句. T.1718.

II. Secondary Sources

Bach, Ulrich E. 2011. "Seeking Emptiness: Theodor Hertzka's Colonial Utopia *Freiland* (1890)," *Utopian Studies*, vol. 22, no. 1, pp. 74–90.

Baker-Smith, Dominic. 2014. "Thomas More," in *The Stanford Encyclopedia of Philosophy*, ed. Edward N. Zalta, https://plato.stanford.edu/archives/spr2014/entries/thomas-more.

Bauer, Wolfgang. 1976. *China and the Search for Happiness: Recurring Themes in Four Thousand Years of Chinese Cultural History*, trans. Michael Shaw. New York: Seabury Press.

Birnbaum, Raoul. 2003. "Buddhist China at the Century's Turn," *The China Quarterly*, no. 174, pp. 428–50.

Cai Zhennian 蔡振念. 2017. "Ren cheng ji fo cheng—Taixu, Yinshun, Xingyun de renjian fojiao"「人成即佛成—太虛、印順、星雲的人間佛教」("The Completion of Humanity is the Completion of Buddhahood—The Humanistic Buddhism of Taixu, Yinshun, and Xingyun"), in *Renjian fojiao de shengming shuxie yu jiaguo guanhuai* 人間佛教的生命書寫與家國關懷, ed. Chen Chienhuang 陳劍鍠. Hong Kong: Zhongwen daxue renjian fojiao yanjiu zhongxin 中文大學人間佛教研究中心, pp. 79–86.

Callahan, Paul E. 1952. "T'ai Hsü and the New Buddhist Movement," *Harvard University Papers on China*, no. 6, pp. 149–88.

Chandler, Stuart. 2004. *Establishing a Pure Land on Earth: The Foguangshan Buddhist Perspective on Modernization and Globalization*. Honolulu: University of Hawai'i Press.

Chen Chienhuang 陳劍鍠. Forthcoming. *Ningshi renjian, beizhi shuangyun: Xingyun dashi de renjian fojiao xingge yu shijian fanxing* 凝視人間,悲智雙運 星雲大師的人間佛教性格與實踐範型. Kaohsiung 高雄: Foguang wenhua shiye youxian gongsi 佛光文化事業有限公司.

Cheng Gongrang 程恭讓. 2015. "Taixu, Shengyan, Xingyun: xiandangdai hanchuan fojiao san daoshi de *Weimoji* quanshi"「太虛、聖嚴、星雲：現當代漢傳佛教三導師的《維摩經》詮釋，」in *Hanchuan fojiao yanjiu de guoqu xianzai weilai* 漢傳佛教研究的過去現在未來, ed. Xie Daning 謝大寧. Ilan 宜蘭: Foguang daxue fojiao yanjiu zhongxin 佛光大學佛教研究中心, pp. 531–610.

Connor, George E. 2000. "The Awakening of Edward Bellamy: Looking Backward at Religious Influence," *Utopian Studies*, vol. 11, no. 1, pp. 38–50.

Ernst, Germana. 2014. "Tommaso Campanella," in *The Stanford Encyclopedia of Philosophy*, ed. Edward N. Zalta, https://plato.stanford.edu/archives/fall2014/entries/campanella.

Fokkema, Douwe. 2011. *Perfect Worlds: Utopian Fiction in China and the West*. Amsterdam: Amsterdam University Press.

Goodell, Eric. 2012. "Taixu's (1890–1947) Creation of Humanistic Buddhism." PhD diss., University of Virginia.

Goossaert, Vincent. 2006. "1898: The Beginning of the End for Chinese Religion?," *Journal of Asian Studies*, vol. 65, no. 2, pp. 307–35.

Graham, A. C., trans. 1990. *The Book of Lieh-tzǔ: A Classic of Tao*. New York: Columbia University Press.

Hertzler, Joyce Oramel. 1923. *The History of Utopian Thought*. London: Macmillan.

Hong Jinlian 洪金蓮. 1999. *Taixu dashi fojiao xiandaihua zhi yanjiu* 太虛大師佛教現代化之研究 (A Study of Taixu's Modernization of Buddhism). Taipei: Fagu wenhua. 法鼓文化.

Hou Kunhong 侯坤宏. 2004. "Cong Taixu dashi dao Yinshun fashi: yi ge sixiangshi jiaodu de guancha"「從太虛大師到印順法師：一個思想史角度的觀察。」. Paper delivered at conference 印順長老與人間佛教, April 24-25, 2004. http://ccbs.ntu.edu.tw/FULLTEXT/JR-NX012/nx117582.pdf, accessed October 3, 2019.

"James Harrington (author)," Wikipedia, https://en.wikipedia.org/wiki/James_Harrington_(author), accessed November 4, 2017.

Jessup, Brooks. 2010. "The Householder Elite: Buddhist Activism in Shanghai, 1920–1956." PhD diss., University of California, Berkeley.

Ji Zhe. 2013. "Zhao Puchu and His Renjian Buddhism," *The Eastern Buddhist*, n.s. vol. 44, no. 2, pp. 35–58.

Jiang Canteng 江燦騰. 1993. *Taixu dashi qianzhuan (1890-1927)* 太虛大師前傳（一八九〇～一九二七）(Taixu's Early Biography, 1890-1927). Taipei: Xinwenfeng 新文豐.

Jiang Canteng 江燦騰. 2009. "Cong jieyan qian dao jieyan hou—zhanhou Yinshun daoshi de renjian jingtu sixiang zai Taiwan de bianqe, zhengbian yu fenhua fazhan"「從解嚴前到解嚴後—戰後印順導師的人間淨土思想在台灣的變革、爭辯與

分化發展」("Before and After the Abolition of Martial Law: The Transformation, Debate and Development of Venerable Yin Shun's 'Thoughts of Pure Land on Earth' in Taiwan after Post War Period (1949))" [sic]), in *Xuanzang fojiao yanjiu* 玄奘佛學研究, vol. 12, pp. 1–28.

Jones, Charles B. 1999. *Buddhism in Taiwan: Religion and the State, 1660–1990.* Honolulu: University of Hawai'i Press.

Jones, Charles B. 2019. *Chinese Pure Land Buddhism: Understanding a Tradition of Practice.* Pure Land Buddhist Studies Series. Honolulu: University of Hawai'i Press.

Jones, Charles B. Forthcoming. "Ven. Taixu's Goal of Establishing the Pure Land in the Human Realm," in *Secularizing Buddhism*, ed. Richard K. Payne. Boston: Shambhala.

Kiely, Jan. 2017. "The Charismatic Monk and the Chanting Masses: Master Yinguang and His Pure Land Revival Movement," in *Making Saints in Modern China*, ed. David Ownby, Vincent Goossaert, and Ji Zhe. New York: Oxford University Press, pp. 30–77.

Klein, Jürgen. 2016. "Francis Bacon," in *The Stanford Encyclopedia of Philosophy*, ed. Edward N. Zalta, https://plato.stanford.edu/archives/win2016/entries/francis-bacon.

Kumar, Krishan. 1987. *Utopia and Anti-utopia in Modern Times.* London: Basil Blackwell.

Levitas, Ruth. 1990. *The Concept of Utopia.* Syracuse: Syracuse University Press.

Li Zhenglong 李政隆 et al. 1990. "Xingzhe tan jianshe renjian jingtu: zuotanhui" 「行者談建設人間淨土：座談會」 ("Practitioners Discuss the Establishment of the Pure Land in the Human Realm: A Symposium"), in *Fojiao wenhua xikan* 佛教文化系刊 (Buddhist Culture), no. 1 (January 1990), pp. 10–16.

Li Zhenglong 李政隆. 1989. "Gongjian renjian jingtu de shehui fuli gongzuo" 「共建人間淨土的福利社會工作」 ("The Task of Benefitting Society by Building the Pure Land in the Human Realm Together"), in *Fojiao wenhua xikan* 佛教文化系刊 (Buddhist Culture), Inaugural Issue (December 1989), p. 2.

Li Zhenglong 李政隆. 1990. "Shenme shi renjian jingtu?" 「什麼是人間淨土？」 ("What Is the Pure Land in the Human Realm?," *Fojiao wenhua xikan* 佛教文化系刊, no. 1, p. 2.

Madsen, Richard. 2007. *Democracy's Dharma: Religious Renaissance and Political Development in Taiwan.* Berkeley: University of California Press.

McRae, John. 1992. "Reconstituting Yōsai (1141–1215): The 'Combined Practice' as an Authentic Interpretation of the Buddhist Tradition," in *1991 Foxue yanjiu lunwen ji 1991* 佛學論文集 (*Anthology of Buddhist Studies*), ed. Kamata Shigeo. 鎌田茂雄 [Kaohsiung]: Foguangshan Publishing 佛光山出版社, pp. 331–424.

Mei Naiwen 梅迺文. 1998. "Cong nüxing zhuyi jiaodu kan renjian jingtu" 「從女性主義角度看人間淨土」 ("Looking at the Pure Land in the Human Realm from a Feminist Perspective"), in *Renjian jingtu yu xiandai shehui* 人間淨土與現代社會, ed. Shi Huimin 釋惠敏. Taipei: Fagu wenhua 法鼓文化, pp. 151–79.

Millican, Frank R. 1923. "T'ai-hsü and Modern Buddhism," *The Chinese Recorder* vol. 54, no. 6, pp. 326–34.

Nedostup, Rebecca. 2009. *Superstitious Regimes: Religion and the Politics of Chinese Modernity.* Harvard East Asian Series 322. Cambridge: Harvard East Asian Center.

Pacey, Scott. 2014. "Taixu, Yogācāra, and the Buddhist Approach to Modernity," in *Transforming Consciousness: Yogācāra Thought in Modern China*, ed. John Makeham. New York: Oxford University Press, pp. 149–69.

Pittman, Don A. 2011. *Toward a Modern Chinese Buddhism: Taixu's Reforms*. Honolulu: University of Hawai'i Press.

Reichelt, Karl Ludwig. 1954. *The Transformed Abbot*. Trans. G. M. Reichelt and A. P. Rose. London: Lutterworth.

Ritzinger, Justin. 2017. *Anarchy in the Pure Land: Reinventing the Cult of Maitreya in Modern Chinese Buddhism*. New York: Oxford University Press.

Tarocco, Francesca. 2007. *The Cultural Practices of Modern Chinese Buddhism*. Routledge Critical Studies in Buddhism. New York: Routledge.

Travagnin, Stefania. 2004. "Master Yinshun and the Pure Land Thought: A Doctrinal Gap between Indian Buddhism and Chinese Buddhism," *Acta Orientalia Academiae Scientiarum Hungaricae*, vol. 57, no. 3, pp. 271–328.

Tymick, Kenneth J. 2014. "The Communist Pure Land: The Legacy of Buddhist Reforms in the Early Chinese Revolutionary Period," *Constructing the Past*: vol. 15, no. 1, Article 10, http://digitalcommons.iwu.edu/constructing/vol15/iss1/10, accessed March 12, 2019.

Wang Jianwei 王建伟. 2010. "Shi xi beifa qianhou Zhongguo Gongchandang dui 'chihua' he 'fanchihua' de pingshu" 试析北伐前后中国共产党对 "赤化" 和 "反赤化" 的评述, *Zhong Gong dang shi yanjiu* 中共党史研究, vol. 4, pp. 45–54.

Welch, Holmes. 1968. *The Buddhist Revival in China*. Harvard East Asian series, 33. Cambridge, MA: Harvard University Press.

Xu, Muzhu 許木柱, Jinhua Chen 陳金華, and Lori Meeks, ed. 2007. *Development and Practice of Humanitarian Buddhism: Interdisciplinary Perspectives*. Hualien: Tzu Chi University.

Yang Huinan 楊惠南. 1991. "Cong 'rensheng fojiao' dao 'renjian fojiao" 從『人生佛教』到『人間佛教』」 ("From 'Buddhism for Human Life' to 'Buddhism for the Human Realm'"), in *Dangdai fojiao sixiang zhanwang* 當代佛教思想展望 (Perspectives on Modern Buddhist Thought). Taipei: Dongda Publishing 東大出版, pp. 75–125.

Yanpei 演培. 1981. "Cong wangsheng jingtu dao shixian renjian jingtu" 「從往生淨土到實現人間淨土」 ("From Rebirth in the Pure Land to Instantiating the Pure Land in the Human Realm"), in *Nanyang fojiao* 南洋佛教, vol. 141, pp. 15–17.

Yinshun 印順. 1992. *Fo zai renjian* 佛在人間 (Buddhas Reside in the Human Realm). Rev. ed. Taipei: Zhengwen Publishing 正聞出版社.

Yinshun 印順. 1992a. *Jingtu yu chan* 淨土與禪 (Pure Land and Chan). Rev. ed. Taipei: Zhengwen Publishing 正聞出版社.

Zamorski, Jakub. 2019. "An Old Savior in a New Paradise: Buddha Amitābha in Tang Dayuan's 'New Pure Land,'" *Journal of Chinese Buddhist Studies*, vol. 32, pp. 97–125.

Zamyatin, Yevgeny. 2006. *We*. Trans. Natasha Randall. New York: Modern Library.

Zhang Longxi. 2002. "The Utopian Vision, East and West," *Utopian Studies*, vol. 13, no. 1, pp. 1–20.

Index

America, migration to 122
Amitābha (buddha) 18–19, 22, 31, 52, 71–2, 112–19
  in relation to Maitreya 53
  vows of 112–18
  see also Amitāyus
Amitāyus 70–2, 74, 77–9, 85, 109–10
  see also Amitābha
anarchism 10–11, 12, 26, 42
Association for the Advancement of Buddhism (Fojiao xiejin hui 佛教協進會) 12
astronomy, modern 121, 142

Bacon, Francis 37, 94, 94 n.22
baihua 白化 see going white
Baizhang 百丈 24
Bauer, Wolfgang 40–1
Bellamy, Edward 37, 41, 60, 60 n.4, 94, 94 n.25
biguan 閉關 see sealed confinement
Birnbaum, Raoul 35
Bodhi Society (Jue she 覺社) 17–18, 40
bodhisattvas 28, 32, 34, 46, 48, 52, 72, 101
Book of the Great Unity (Datong shu 大同書) 10
buddha recollection see nianfo
Buddha's Light International Association 131, 132
Buddhism for Human Life (rensheng fojiao 人生佛教) 24, 129, 129 n.1
Buddhism for the Human Realm (renjian fojiao 人間佛教) 129, 129 n.1
Buddhist Association of China 139
Buddhist community, Taixu's plan for 15, 24, 43–5, 48, 94 n.23, 98–101, 135
  eight schools of Buddhism in 98–9, 101
  governance of 100–1
  land distribution in 43–4, 99
  missions abroad from 48, 100, 101
  monastic training in 99
  relations with outside world 100–1

Buddhist Culture (magazine; Fojiao wenhua 佛教文化) 20, 136–7
buddha-recitation see nianfo
Butler, Samuel 46

Cai Zhennian 蔡振念 35
Callahan, Paul 32, 144
Campanella, Tommaso 37, 94, 94 n.23
Case Studies of Datong in the East (Dongfang datong xue'an 東方大同學案) 27, 40–1, 87 n.12
Chen Duxiu 142
Chiang Kai-shek 28
chihua 赤化 see going red
China: current conditions in 16, 27–8, 122
Chinese Buddhist Federation (Zhonghua fojiao lianhehui 中華佛教聯合會) 25
Chinese Communist Party 138–9
Chinese Socialist Party 12, 13
Christianity 24, 136
  contrast with Buddhism 136
City of the Sun 37, 94, 94 n.23
civil examination system 7, 8, 22
class struggle 45, 58, 58 n.1, 79–80, 93
Commonwealth of Oceania 37, 94, 94 n.24
Communism 47, 93 n.14
Communists, Chinese 28
confiscation of temple properties 10–11
Confucius 94
conflict, causes of 50–1, 57–8, 79–80
consciousness-only see mind-only
contemporary problems 20, 50–1, 78–80, 87, 122
cosmology, Buddhist 22, 49–51, 58 n.2, 132, 142
creation by a deity 123

Da nao Jinshan 大鬧金山 see "Invasion of Jinshan"
Daan (大安, 1959–) 138

Dalin Temple (*Dalin si* 大林寺) 25
Daoism 8
Daojie (道階, 1866–1934) 9
Datong shu 大同書 *see* Book of the Great Unity
Datong 大同 *see* Great Unity
Datongshi 大同世 *see* World of Great Unity
death 34, 44, 45, 52
dependent recompense (*yi bao* 依報) 50, 57
Dharma Drum Mountain (*Fagu shan* 法鼓山) 135
Dharmākara, practices of 112, 118–19
  vows of 112–18
  see also Amitābha
Dongfang datong xue'an 東方大同學案 *see* Case Studies of Datong in the East
Dongya fojiao dahui 東亞佛教大會 *see* Great East Asian Buddhist Conference
Dongya fojiao lianhehui 東亞佛教聯合會 *see* East Asian Buddhist Federation
Dostoyevsky, Fyodor 47

East Asian Buddhist Federation (*Dongya fojiao lianhehui* 東亞佛教聯合會) 25
education 16, 17, 18, 22, 46, 67, 124, 135
Eight Fingers *see* Jichan
Eight schools of Buddhism 14–15, 17, 32, 98–9, 101, 143
Eisai (栄西, 1141–1215) 143–4
Erewhon 46
esoteric rituals 4, 32, 97–9, 143
eugenics 43, 67

Fagu shan see Dharma Drum Mountain
feminism 136
First World War 13
Five Defilements 121
Five Evils 80–6
Five Kinds of Burning 80–6, 112
Five Kinds of Pain 80–6, 112
Five Lay Precepts 105, 132
  village 43, 99
Fo Kuang Shan *see* Foguang Shan
Foguang Pure Land (*Foguang jingtu* 佛光淨土) 132–3
Foguang Shan 佛光山 131, 132

Fojiao wenhua see Buddhist Culture
Fojiao xiejin hui 佛教協進會 *see* Association for the Advancement of Buddhism
Fokkema, Douwe 39, 42
Four Eminent Monks 3, 14, 144
Freeland: A Social Anticipation 37, 94, 94 n.26

going red (*chihua* 赤化) 20, 45, 58, 58 n.1, 79–80, 93
going white (*baihua* 白化) 58, 58 n.1, 79–80
Goodell, Eric 9, 14, 14 n.1, 18, 22, 33–4
government 10, 12, 26, 35, 45, 93, 100, 133
  and Buddhism 10–11, 13, 21, 25–6, 35, 38, 101, 124, 133
  and the Pure Land in the Human Realm 93, 100, 101, 124
Great East Asian Buddhist Conference (*Dongya fojiao dahui* 東亞佛教大會, 1925) 26–7
Great Leap Forward 138–9
Great Unity (*Datong* 大同) 43, 63, 64, 66, 67, 68, 89, 94
Guomindang see Nationalist Party

Haichaoyin 海潮音 (magazine) 18–20
Hamilton, Clarence 25, 32
Harrington, James 37, 94, 94 n.24
Hertzka, Theodor 37, 94, 94 n.26
Hertzler, Joyce 40–1
HONG Jinlian 洪金蓮 36
Hongyi (弘一, 1880–1942) 3
Huashan (華山, 1870–1918) 10–11
Huayan Sutra (*Huayan jing* 華嚴經) 9, 132
human realm (*renjian* 人間) 49–50
Humanistic Science (*Renshengguan de kexue* 人生觀的科學) 23, 34

idealism 123
imperialism 58, 58 n.1
INADA Ensai 稻田圓成 25
industry 124
Inner Court of Maitreya 16, 39, 44, 45, 52, 53, 102–8
  subsumed in the Pure Land of the Ocean of Awakening 111
  see also Tuṣita Heaven

"Invasion of Jinshan" (*da nao Jinshan* 大鬧金山) 12–13, 27

Jambudvīpa 58, 69, 70, 78, 106–7
Japan 17
    Taixu's trips to 17, 24–7
Japanese Buddhism 10–11, 17
Japanese Buddhist missionaries 10–11, 17
Japanese invasion of China 28
Jessup, Brooks 36
Jesus 93
Jetavana Hermitage (*Zhihuan jingshe* 祇洹精舍), Nanjing 11
JIANG Canteng 江燦騰 9, 13, 29, 35–6
Jichan (寄禪, 1852–1912) 9, 10, 11, 13
Jingci Temple 淨慈寺 22
Jinshan Monastery (*Jinshan si* 金山寺) 12
    see also "Invasion of Jinshan"
Jue she 覺社 see Bodhi Society
Juehai jingtu 覺海淨土 see Pure Land of the Ocean of Awakening

KANG Youwei (康有為, 1858–1927) 10
Kitagawa, Joseph 33
Korean War 138–9
Kropotkin, Peter (1842–1921) 19, 67
Kumar, Krishan 47
Kuo Min Tang see Nationalist Party

Land of Utmost Bliss see Pure Land
Land Reform Movement 32, 138–9
Lao Dan 老聃 41, 86
Laozi 93
Larger Sukhāvatī-vyūha-sūtra 70–8, 80–6, 112–19
lecture halls, urban 18, 21, 23
LI Zhenglong 李政隆 136–7
Liaoyu 了餘 9, 14
Liezi 列子 41, 86–7, 94, 94 n.15, 94 n.16, 94 n.17
LIU Renhang (劉仁航, 1884–1938) 18, 20, 27, 40–1
Looking Backward, 2000-1887 37, 41, 60, 94, 94 n.25
    in Japanese translation 60 n.4
LÜ Gansen 呂淦森 see Taixu
Lushan Huiyuan (廬山慧遠, 334–416) 15–16

Madsen, Richard 32

Maitreya 39, 52, 55, 137
    contemplation of 105, 108
    prediction of future buddhahood 102–8
    in relation to Amitābha 53
    return to present world and attainment of buddhahood 106, 107, 108, 137, 138
    Taixu's devotion to 34, 53
    Yinshun's views on 130
Marx, Karl 46, 93 n.14
Marxism 43, 45, 58 n.1, 93, 93 n.14
materialism 26, 78–9, 93, 123
May Fourth Movement 18
McRae, John 143–4
MEI Naiwen 梅迺文 136
Mencius (*Mengzi* 孟子, c. 372–289 BCE) 94
Millican, Frank R. 25, 31–2
mind, primacy of 123
mind-only (*weixin* 唯心) 14, 134
mind-only Pure Land (*weixin jingtu* 唯心淨土) 134, 135, 137, 141
    in relation to other forms of Pure Land 134–5
Mingjing 明鏡 8
Modern Utopia, A 37, 94–5, 95 n.27
monastic community (*sangha*)
    in the Pure Land 95–6
    reform of 3, 14, 16, 18, 20, 22, 32, 35
    state of 3, 9, 20
More, Thomas 37, 94, 94 n.21
mountaintop community see Buddhist community

Nanjing Decade 28
Nationalist Party (*Guomindang* 國民黨) 138
natural disasters 26, 51, 78–9, 112
New Culture Movement 18
New Pure Land (*xin jingtu* 新淨土) 18–19, 21, 138
New Villages 19
nianfo 念佛 18–19, 22, 27, 31, 32, 36, 45, 133–4
Northern Expedition 28, 33
Nova Atlantis 37, 94 n.22

On Benevolence (*Renxue* 仁學) 10
offerings, necessity of 118, 120

optimists 123, 137, 141
other planets 49, 51, 95 n.27, 142

PANG Yun 龐蘊 24
paradises as distinct from utopias 38–9, 47
People's Republic of China 138–9
pessimists 123, 137, 141
philosophy of human life (*rensheng guan* 人生觀), debates on 23
Pilu Monastery (*Pilu si* 比盧寺) 12
Pittman, Don A. 33
planets *see* other planets
Plato 37, 94
pratyekabuddhas 23, 72, 113
prayer 97–8
proper recompense (*zheng bao* 正報) 50, 57
Proposal for Institutional Reform in the Sangha (*Zhengli sengqie zhidu lun* 整理僧伽制度論) 14, 16, 32
Pure Land 39, 44, 50, 53, 70–8, 79, 85, 109–10
  attributes of 70–8, 109–10, 134
  compatible with reform work 51–2, 133–4, 138, 142
  meaning of 79
  in the People's Republic of China 138–9
  rebirth in 19, 24, 44, 45, 52, 57, 71, 77–8, 101, 110, 134
  subsumed in the Pure Land of the Ocean of Awakening 111, 134
  see also Sukhāvatī, Land of Utmost Bliss
Pure Land in the Human Realm (*renjian jingtu* 人間淨土) 4, 21, 24, 129
  as both utopia and paradise 39, 44–5, 93
  and feminism 136
  means of creating 93–6, 112, 120–5, 137, 138
  Sheng Yen's ideas for 133–5
  subsumed in the Pure Land of the Ocean of Awakening 111
  Xingyun's ideas for 131–3
Pure Land of the Ocean of Awakening (*Juehai jingtu* 覺海淨土) 52, 53, 111, 132, 134
Pure Land School 15–16
pure lands (as a generic term) 49, 85, 102, 120–2
  causes of 121–2

Putuo, Mount (*Putuo shan* 普陀山) 13–14, 17, 98
Putuo shan see Putuo, Mount

Qiyun (棲雲, d.u.) 10–11

Reichelt, Karl Ludwig 4, 31
renjian 人間; *see* Human Realm
renjian jingtu 人間淨土 *see* Pure Land in the Human Realm
Renshan (仁山, 1887–1951) 12
Renshengguan de kexue 人生觀的科學 *see* Humanistic Science
Renxue 仁學 *see On Benevolence*
Ritzinger, Justin 10, 34, 93 n.14

Saint-Simon, Comte de 93
Śākyamuni Buddha 98, 99
Sangha Education Association (*Seng[jia] jiaoyu hui* 僧[伽]教育會) 11
Sangha Normal School (*Seng shifan xuetang* 僧師範學堂), Nanjing 11
sangha see monastic community
Schak, David 34
science 23, 26, 79, 94 n.22, 123
science and Buddhism 23, 51, 58, 121, 123, 142
sealed confinement (*biguan* 閉關) 13–6
Seng shifan xuetang 僧師範學堂 *see* Sangha Normal School
Seng[jia] jiaoyu hui 僧[伽]教育會 *see* Sangha Education Association
Shanhui (善慧, 1881–1945) 17
Sheng Yen (*Shengyan* 聖嚴, 1930–2009) 133–5, 139, 142
Shengyan see Sheng Yen
Shida 士達 8
Shijie fojiao lianhehui 世界佛教聯合會 *see* World Buddhist Federation
shishan 十善 *see* Ten Virtues
Shuangxi Temple (*Shuangxi si* 雙溪寺) 11
socialism 10–11, 26, 93
Socrates 37, 94
solar system 51, 58, 70, 142
Sound of the Ocean Tide see Haichaoyin
śrāvakas 72, 75, 76, 113
Sukhāvatī 16, 34, 39, 46, 53, 72, 101, 131, 133, 134, 135, 142

see also Pure Land, Land of
   Utmost Bliss
supernatural powers (*shentong* 神通) 8,
   22, 143
Sutra on the Arising of Worlds (*Qishi
   yinben jing* 起世因本經, T.24), 41,
   42, 45–6, 58–70

T'ai-hsü *see* Taixu
Taiwan 16–17, 20
Taixu (太虛, 1890–1947)
   as abbot 11, 22
   birth and family 7–8
   Buddhist organizing 12
   early apprenticeship 7–8
   early monastic career 9
   early schooling 7
   grandmother's influence 7–8, 33
   influences on his thought 18–21
   involvement with anarchism and
      socialism 10–11, 12, 27, 31, 42, 46
   and Japanese Buddhism 16–17, 24–7
   Maitreya devotion 16, 34, 43
   modern scholarly views on 4, 31–6
   ordination 8–9
   publishing activities 11, 18
   reform work 21–2, 27
   relations with government 11, 12, 25, 35
   religious experiences 9, 14
   sealed confinement 13–16
   search for supernatural powers 8, 22
   self-assessment 120
   and technology 46
   travels abroad 17, 26–7
Tan Sitong (譚嗣同, 1865–1898) 10
Tang Dayuan (唐大圓, 1890–1941)
   18–20, 28, 138, 139
Tantric Buddhism, popularity of 16
   see also esoteric rituals
technological futurism 42
technology 46, 79
   related to Buddhist paradises 42, 43, 61,
      68, 131
   as solution to human problems 46, 79
temple confiscation measures 10–11
Ten Virtues (*shishan* 十善) 43, 44, 51, 58,
   69, 97, 99, 100, 101, 102, 138
   village 99
Thailand 98

Three Refuges 44, 46, 99, 102
   village 99
Tiantong Monastery (*Tiantong
   si* 天童寺) 8
Tibet 98
Tolstoy, Leo 93
Tongshan she 同善社 *see* Uniform Virtue
   Society
Tuṣita Heaven 16, 39, 45, 102–8
   deities of 105
   gaining rebirth in 45, 104, 105, 107–8
   Maitreya's ascent to 102–8
   subsumed in the Pure Land of the
      Ocean of Awakening 11
   Yinshun's views on 130–1

Uniform Virtue Society (*Tongshan she*
   同善社) 17
urban laity 23, 36
   Taixu's focus on 16, 18, 21, 23–4, 36
Utmost Bliss, Land of *see* Pure Land
Utopia 37, 94, 94 n.21
utopias 38, 47
   as distinct from paradises 38–9, 47
Uttarakuru 4, 38, 39, 41–3, 45–6, 49–50,
   51, 54, 57–70, 79, 88, 93, 96, 131, 135,
   135 n.3, 142
   causes of rebirth in 45, 51, 69, 96–7
   description of 41–3, 51, 58–70
   lifespan in 47, 51, 68–9, 70

Vairocana Buddha 98
Vimalakīrti Sūtra 18, 137
vows, necessity of 120

war 28, 50–1, 58, 79–80
warlords 16, 27, 28
We (book by Zamyatin) 40
weixin 唯心 *see* mind-only
Welch, Holmes 33
Wells, H. G. 37, 94–5, 95 n.27
western-direction Pure Land (*xifang jingtu*
   西方淨土) 134–5
   in relation to other forms of Pure
      Land 134–5
World Buddhist Federation (*Shijie fojiao
   lianhehui* 世界佛教聯合會) 24–5
World of Great Unity (*Datongshi* 大同世)
   63, 64 66–8

Xiao Jiuhuashan monastery (*Xiao jiuhuashan si* 小九華山寺) 8, 10
Xifang Temple (*Xifang si* 西方寺) 9
Xingyun (星雲, 1927–) 131–3, 139
  and Foguang Pure Land 132–3
Xuyun (虛雲, 1840–1959) 3

yi bao 依報 *see* dependent recompense
Yinguang (印光, 1861–1940) 3, 13–14, 18
  relations with Taixu 13–14
Yinshun (印順, 1906–2005) 129–31, 139
  on three types of Pure Land 130
  view of traditional Pure Land 130
Yongfeng Chan Monastery (*Yongfeng chanyuan* 永豐禪院) 9
Yongming Yanshou (永明延壽, 904–975) 22
Yōsai *see* Eisai

Young East, The (journal) 26
Yuan Shikai, President 13, 16
Yuanying (圓瑛, 1878–1953) 9, 16

Zamorski, Jakub 18
Zamyatin, Evgeny 40
Zang Guanchan (藏貫禪) 20–1, 28, 97, 97 n.28, 132
Zhang Longxi 39
Zhang Taiyan (章太炎, 1869–1936) 10
Zhao Puchu (趙樸初, 1907–2000) 139
zheng bao 正報 *see* proper recompense
Zhihuan jingshe 祇洹精舍 *see* Jetavana Hermitage
Zhonghua fojiao lianhehui 中華佛教聯合會 *see* Chinese Buddhist Federation
Zhuangzi 莊子 (c. 369–286 BCE) 93

www.ingramcontent.com/pod-product-compliance
Lightning Source LLC
Chambersburg PA
CBHW070642300426
44111CB00013B/2226